Mary,
Mary

Also by Jean Kerr:

THE SNAKE HAS ALL THE LINES

PLEASE DON'T EAT THE DAISIES

Plays:

GOLDILOCKS (*with Walter Kerr*)

KING OF HEARTS

Barbara Bel Geddes as Mary.

Mary, Mary

by

Jean Kerr

DOUBLEDAY & COMPANY, INC.

GARDEN CITY, NEW YORK

1963

All photographs from Friedman-Abeles

All of the characters in this book are fictitious, and any resemblance to actual persons, living or dead, is purely coincidental.

LIBRARY OF CONGRESS CATALOG CARD NUMBER 61–13804   COPYRIGHT ©
1960, 1961, 1963, BY JEAN KERR   ALL RIGHTS RESERVED   PRINTED IN
THE UNITED STATES OF AMERICA

For Walter,
who insisted that I write this play
even when I knew better.

Setting

The action takes place in BOB McKELLAWAY's living room, which is also an office away from the office, in a New York apartment building. The place is well kept, and obviously belongs to a man of taste and intelligence, but it is neither chic nor overly expensive. When the lights are lowered, it has a cozy, domestic feel to it, as though it had already been shared with a woman, though Bob is a bachelor at the moment and has let his homework rather overrun the place. He is a publisher by profession, heading his own small company, and he has a cluttered desk at one side of the room. Otherwise the customary sofa, chairs, liquor cabinet, bookshelves, a fish tank, and so on. There are entrances to five other areas: a main door to the outside corridor, a door to the bedroom, one to the kitchen, one to a linen closet, and one to what is obviously a cubbyhole filled with business files.

Characters

BOB MCKELLAWAY   a young independent publisher
                         in his thirties.

MARY MCKELLAWAY   his former wife, divorced within
                         the year and now working on
                         her own.

TIFFANY RICHARDS   Bob's present fiancée, in
                         her twenties, independently
                         wealthy.

OSCAR NELSON   a tax lawyer and a friend of
                         both Bob and Mary. Fiftyish.

DIRK WINSTON   recently from Hollywood, and a
                         wartime friend of Bob.

ACT ONE

A Saturday morning in winter.

ACT TWO

Saturday night, late.

ACT THREE

Sunday morning.

Act One

AT RISE: Bob *is on the telephone. Several morning news-papers, open to the book page, are spread out in front of him. He dials a number.*

BOB

I want to speak to Mr. Howard Nieman.
        (*The doorbell rings once, perfunctorily*)
Okay, I'll hold on.

TIFFANY
        (*Letting herself in at the front door; she carries a jar of wheat germ*)
Bob!

BOB

Hi, honey.

TIFFANY
        (*Leaving the door ajar and coming into the room apprehensively*)
I've read the reviews. How are you feeling?

1

BOB

I'm not exactly dancing with glee.

TIFFANY

Well, it's not fair!

BOB
(*Rising, phone in hand*)
Shhhh! This is Nieman. I'm waiting for him to get off the other line.

TIFFANY
(*Coming to* BOB *at the desk*)
But it isn't fair. You publish books of quality and distinction and you should get the credit.

BOB

You're one hundred percent correct and beautiful besides.
(*They kiss*)

(*Into the phone*)
Hello, Howard! How are you?
(*He sits, pulling newspapers toward him*)
Yes, sure I read the notices. Well, Howard, we were both hoping for a better break, but on the other hand there are a lot of good quotes here.
(*Running his finger down a page and having some difficulty finding a decent quote*)
"A magician with words" and so forth.
(TIFFANY *hangs her coat on the railing, and quietly feeds wheat germ to the fish*)
And with a book like yours we can hope for something more in the weeklies. I'm confident we'll go into another printing.

2

Act One

What did you think about the notices? Sure, we all wish Orville Prescott would write a novel. Look, Howard, please calm down. I hope you're not going around talking this way. Well, for one thing, people don't read reviews that carefully. All you do is spread the bad word.
> (*Rises, fidgeting*)

Let me give you some advice from Jake Cooper, in publicity. In his coarse but memorable phrase, nobody knows you've got a boil on your behind if you don't tell them.
> (BOB *listens a second longer, then shrugs and hangs up*)

TIFFANY

What did he say?

BOB

He said the boil was not on his behind.
> (*Picks up a newspaper*)

It was on page 34 of the New York *Times.*

TIFFANY

Why shouldn't he be mad? It's a wonderful book!

BOB

That's what I like. Loyalty.
> (*Suddenly remembering, picking up a box of candy*)

I have a present for you and I forgot about it.

TIFFANY

A present?

BOB

It's Valentine's Day.
(*Bringing her the box*)
Did you forget? To the sweet. Will you be my valentine?
(*Kiss*)

TIFFANY

Sure I'll be your valentine.
(*Pulls* BOB *down onto the sofa. He is kissing her as* OSCAR *appears from the corridor with a brief case*)

OSCAR

(*Pushing the door wider*)
The door is open. Shall I come in?

BOB

Oh, Oscar—by all means. Tiffany, I want you to meet Oscar Nelson. My old friend and my new tax lawyer.

TIFFANY

Hello.

BOB

And this is Tiffany Richards. We're getting married next month.

OSCAR

And she'll be deductible.
(*Comes down to shake hands with* TIFFANY)
Congratulations.
(BOB *closes the door*)

4

TIFFANY

Well, I'm very happy he's got you as a tax lawyer. Don't you think it's just outrageous—the government investigating his back taxes just like he was Frank Sinatra?

OSCAR

Under the law we're all equals.

BOB

Oscar—think of that clunk from the FBI who came charging in here and accused me of fleecing the government of six thousand dollars!

OSCAR

Wait, wait, wait. In the first place, this clunk is not from the FBI. He's from the Internal Revenue Service, a small but real distinction. In the second place, he is not accusing you of anything. He is merely asking you to produce proof that this six thousand dollars was legitimate professional expenses.

BOB

All I can tell you is that I am not coughing up any six thousand dollars. I'll move to Alaska.

OSCAR

You're too late. It's come into the Union.

TIFFANY

Darling, there's nothing to be upset about. Mr. Nelson will handle this man.
(*Rises*)

Now *I'm* going to get you your midafternoon cocktail.
> (*To* OSCAR)
Would you like one?

OSCAR

Not this early, thank you.

TIFFANY

It's not alcohol. It's raw milk, brewer's yeast, and wheat germ.

OSCAR

Not this early, thank you.

BOB
> (*Aware of* OSCAR'S *expression*)
It does sound awful, but it's incredible the energy it gives you.

OSCAR

I'll have to try it sometime.

TIFFANY

You have no intention of trying it. And you know what? You should, because you're definitely undernourished. Look at your ears.

OSCAR

What about them? I know they stick out.

TIFFANY

They're whitish. Here, let me look at your fingernails.
> (*She picks up his hand*)
See how pale they are? A really healthy person will have pink

6

ears and pink fingernails. Another thing—a healthy person will have a tongue the color of beefsteak.

OSCAR
(Backing away, hand to mouth)
No, no—I will spare you that.

TIFFANY
I'm going to bring you a cocktail, and you try it.
(She goes off to the kitchen and closes the door)

BOB
You think that's a lot of damn nonsense.

OSCAR
How did you know?

BOB
Because that's what I thought, in the beginning. But I have seen the results and I am completely sold. And if you want to know—I *love* being clucked over.

OSCAR
I'm delighted to hear it. And your ears were never lovelier. Now, shall we get down to business?
(Goes to the desk with his brief case)

BOB
Please, let's. I'm in a real mess, Oscar. Actually, it's been a muddle ever since I started to pay alimony. And now this tax thing. What am I going to do? You probably read those notices today. I won't make anything on the Nieman book.

Somewhere, something's got to give. And it's got to be straightened out before Tiffany and I get married.

OSCAR
(Spreading out various papers on the desk)
We'll see what we can do.

BOB
What I want is a bird's-eye view of my whole financial picture. What I'm spending. What I should be spending. Where I should be cutting corners.

OSCAR
All right. I've already come to a few conclusions, but I'll want to look at your files—
(Makes a gesture toward the inner office)

BOB
Thanks, Oscar. And I appreciate your coming over here on a Saturday. In fact, I appreciate your taking on this whole dumb job. I didn't think you would.

OSCAR
Why not?

BOB
Well,
(Glancing toward the kitchen door)
you wouldn't handle the divorce.

OSCAR
Bob, how could I have handled the divorce? Mary was just as much my friend as you were. Besides, I never thought you'd

8

go through with it. I thought of you as the golden couple—
smiling over steaming bowls of Campbell's chicken soup—

BOB

Oh, brother.

OSCAR

What happened?

BOB
(*With a shrug*)
What happens to any marriage. You're in love, and then
you're not in love. I married Mary because she was so direct
and straightforward and said just exactly what she meant.

OSCAR

And why did you divorce her?

BOB

Because she was so direct and straightforward and said just
exactly what she meant.

OSCAR

When did you see her last?

BOB

Eight, nine months ago.

OSCAR

Well, you're going to see her this afternoon.

BOB

Like hell!

OSCAR

Bob, I called Mary in Philadelphia and asked her—as a special favor—to come up here this afternoon.

BOB

But why would you do that? Why in God's name would you—?

OSCAR

Why? Because you have five thousand dollars' worth of canceled checks that you can neither identify nor explain. Some of them Mary signed. I'm hoping that her memory will be a little better than yours.

BOB
(*Searching for an out*)
But I've got an appointment here in ten minutes. Do you remember Dirk Winston?

OSCAR

The movie actor? Sure.

BOB

We were in the Navy together. Now he's moved into this building.

OSCAR

Well, it's nice you two old sailors can get together. There ought to be many a salty story, many a hearty laugh.

BOB

You don't get the picture. He's written a book.

10

Act One

A book?

BOB

That's right. The story of his life in three hundred and eighteen ungrammatical pages.
> (*Hands him a manuscript from the low bookcase*)

OSCAR
> (*Glancing at it*)

Life Among the Oranges. Not a bad title.

BOB

It's all right, I suppose.
> (*Picks up a small bowl of dried apricots and begins to eat one, nervously*)

I can't imagine it on our lists.

OSCAR

I gather you're not going to do it.

BOB

Of course I'm not going to do it. But I dread talking to him. There is no right way to tell an author you don't want to publish his book.

OSCAR

If it's not going to be sweet, make it short. I can take Mary into the office—

BOB

Oh—Mary.
(*Suddenly turning on* OSCAR)
Don't you leave me alone with her for one minute, do you hear?

OSCAR

She's only five feet three.

BOB

Never mind that.
(*Going to the file cabinet, upset, and picking up a set of galleys*)
And when will I get to these galleys? They have to be back to the printer on Monday.

OSCAR

What are you eating?

BOB

Dried apricots.
(OSCAR *remains silent*)
They're full of vitamin C.

OSCAR

The things I'm learning today!
(*Indicating the galleys* BOB *is fretting over*)
What's that one like?

BOB

It's absolutely fascinating. I want you to read it.
(*Enthusing, partly to distract himself*)

Act One

It's told in the first person, and when the story opens we're coming back from a funeral. But only gradually do we come to realize that the narrator of the story is the dead man.

OSCAR

It sounds sensitive, very sensitive.

BOB

(*An extravagant little flare-up*)
Oscar, I can think of only one sure way to clean up in this business! A new series. I could take the great sex novels—*Lady Chatterley, Peyton Place*—and have them rewritten for the ten-to-twelve age group.
(TIFFANY *enters with drinks, bringing one to* BOB)

TIFFANY

It took me longer because the Waring Blendor was broken. . . .

BOB

Thank you, darling.

TIFFANY

And I had to use an egg beater.
(*Handing a glass to* OSCAR, *who rises*)
You've *got* to *taste* it, anyway.
(*He doesn't*)

BOB

(*Taking over*)
Honey, I want you to put on your new gray bonnet and get out of here.

TIFFANY

(*Surprised*)

Bob! Aren't we driving up to Goshen? Dad's expecting us!

BOB

Certainly. I'll pick you up at five-thirty. No, make it six.

TIFFANY

(*Really puzzled*)

But why do I have to *go*?

BOB

Because in my winning, boyish way, I'm asking you to.

TIFFANY

I know why! Because that sexy movie actor is coming. You think in ten minutes I'll be sitting on his lap giving little growls of rapture.

BOB

Nonsense. Why should you care about vulgar good looks when you have me? No—

(*With a sigh and moving away from her*)

—the truth is my ex-wife is descending upon me this afternoon.

OSCAR

It was my suggestion. I thought she might be able to shed some light on this tax matter.

TIFFANY

(*Abruptly*)

14

I'm delighted. I want to meet her. I've always wanted to meet her.

BOB

Well, you're not *going* to meet her—

TIFFANY
(*Sitting down, firmly, in a chair*)

Yes, I am.

(Oscar, *sensing that he'd better, slips away into the inner office with his papers and closes the door*)

BOB

Darling, you are a sweet, reasonable girl, and I insist that you stay in character. Besides, I have those galleys to finish.
(*As though to conclude the matter*)
Kiss me, and stop all this nonsense.

TIFFANY
(*Deliberately refusing to move*)

I won't. I am not going to turn into Joan Fontaine.

BOB

What the hell are you talking about?

TIFFANY

Don't you remember Joan Fontaine in *Rebecca?* She was always thinking about the first Mrs. de Winter. She used to imagine that she could see her ghost on the staircase with that straight black Indian hair floating out behind her. Don't you remember? And she'd shudder when she saw the monogram on the silver brushes.

15

BOB

(*With a snort*)

Silver brushes! Mary used to use plastic combs with little tails, and she'd crack off the tails so they'd fit in her purse. And her hair was tied back in a bun. Tiffany—this is so silly!

TIFFANY

I'll tell you another reason why I ought to meet Mary. We'd probably have a lot in common. Daddy says that a man goes on making the same mistake indefinitely.

BOB

Is that supposed to be an epigram? Because I don't get it.

TIFFANY

Practically everybody Daddy knows is divorced. It's not that they're worse than other people, they're just richer. And you do begin to see the pattern. You know Howard Pepper. When he divorced his first wife, everybody said "Oh, what he endured with Maggie! It was hell on earth!" Then when he married the new girl, everybody said "She's so *good* for him." Except when you met her she looked like Maggie, she talked like Maggie, it was Maggie all over again. And now his *third* wife—

BOB

Okay, okay. I get the whole ghastly picture. But I promise you on my sacred oath as a Yale man that you don't resemble my ex-wife in any way, shape, or form.

TIFFANY

Is that good?

BOB

(*Relaxing for a moment with* TIFFANY *on the sofa*)

Good? It's a benediction from heaven. You—sweet, idiot child —soothe my feathers. Mary always, always ruffled them. Life with Mary was like being in a phone booth with an open umbrella—no matter which way you turned, you got it in the eye.

TIFFANY

Well, at last—a plain statement! Now that you've opened up a little, tell me, where did you meet her? Who introduced you?

BOB

I don't think we *were* introduced.

TIFFANY

You picked her up.

BOB

In a way. Do you remember that novel we published—*Our Kingdom Come?* It was sort of an allegory—the pilot of the plane turned out to be God?

TIFFANY

I don't think so.

BOB

Well, they made a play out of it. So of course I had to go to the opening night. And it was awful. Really grisly. After the second act, we were all standing out on the sidewalk. We were too stunned to talk. In fact, there didn't seem to be anything to say. Finally this girl spoke. She was standing there by herself in a polo coat, smoking—and she said, "Well, it's *not* uneven." So I laughed, and we started to talk—

TIFFANY

And you said, "We don't have to go back in there, let's have a drink—"

BOB

See? I don't have to tell you. You know.
(*Rises and gets her coat*)

TIFFANY

(*Rising, too, pursuing the subject*)
Did you kiss her that night?

BOB

Come on. Put on your coat. You're just stalling for time.

TIFFANY

I'll bet you did.

BOB

What?

TIFFANY

Kiss her that night.

BOB

I didn't kiss her for weeks.

TIFFANY

I don't believe it. You kissed me on the second night—in the elevator—do you remember?

BOB

(*Thinking of* MARY)

Oh, I made certain fumbling attempts—but she'd make some little joke, like "Let's not start something we can't finish in a cab on Forty-fourth Street"—

TIFFANY

Well, for goodness sake, where was she when you finally did kiss her? On an operating table, under ether?

BOB

No, as it happens she was in a cab on Forty-fourth Street. Somehow or other she got her fingers slammed in the door. She pretended it was nothing, and we were chatting along. Then suddenly—this was blocks later—she started to cry. I looked at her fingers.

(*Taking* TIFFANY's *hand*)

Two of the nails were really smashed. And it started out I was just trying to comfort her, and—

TIFFANY

That is the most *un*romantic story I ever heard!

BOB

They certainly won't get a movie out of it.

(*Urging her toward door*)

I told you it wasn't worth discussing.

TIFFANY
(Picks up her handbag)
I know, I kept fishing. Did she cry a lot in taxicabs?

BOB
She never cried again. Not anyplace—ever—not once.
(Oscar appears from inner office, frowning over a sheaf of papers)

OSCAR
These figures for the year—can they represent the *total* profit?

BOB
I'm afraid so.
(Doorbell. Bob thinks quickly)
Oscar, will you get that?

TIFFANY
Just let me *meet* her. Two minutes and I promise I'll go!

BOB
(Pulling her toward the kitchen)
We'll go out the back door and I'll get you a cab.

TIFFANY
I feel like I was caught in a raid!
(Oscar has been looking on as Bob gets Tiffany into the kitchen)

BOB
I'm *not* adult and Noel Coward would wash his hands of me.
(He slips into the kitchen, too, and closes the

Act One

> *door as* OSCAR *crosses to the main door and*
> *opens it not to* MARY *but to* DIRK WINSTON,
> *who has a large, partially wrapped piece of wood*
> *carving in his arms*)

OSCAR

Hello. Come in.

DIRK

I'm—

OSCAR

Yes, I know. You're Dirk Winston. Bob will be right back. My
name is Oscar Nelson.
> (*We hear* TIFFANY *giggling and protesting*
> *"Please, Bob—please!" off in the kitchen area.*
> OSCAR *and* DIRK *hear it, too*)
Her name is Tiffany Richards.
> (*Squeals from* TIFFANY, *off*)

DIRK

It kind of makes me homesick for the back lot at Paramount.
I thought I was late, but . . .
> (OSCAR, *puzzled, is looking at the package in*
> DIRK's *arms*)
Suppose I take this thing downstairs and I'll be back in ten
minutes.

OSCAR

I think recess should be over by that time.

DIRK
(Feeling he should explain the package)
I saw this in an antique shop.
(Undoing the wrapping a bit)
It's supposed to be Geronimo, but it looks so much like Jack Warner I couldn't resist.

> *(He goes, closing the door. Oscar notices the drink Tiffany has left for him. He tastes it, then crosses to the liquor table and pours a generous slug into the drink. He takes a sip. It's better. He looks at his fingernails, then goes to the mantel, puts down his drink, picks up a mirror, and examines his tongue. While he is doing so, Mary enters by the main door. She puts down her overnight bag and then sees Oscar.)*

MARY
Oscar!

OSCAR
Mary, darling.

MARY
Are you sick?

OSCAR
Of course not. I'm out of my mind.
(Going to her and embracing her)
Hey! I want you to concentrate and give me a better hug than that!

> *(We are aware that Mary is somewhat abstracted and apprehensive. Also that she is get-*

22

Act One

   ting her feel of the room again, after all this
   time)

MARY

Oscar—dear Oscar—it's lovely to see you.
   (*Hesitantly*)
Where's—?

OSCAR

He'll be right back. He just—
   (*Interrupting himself, staring at her*)
Wait a minute! What's happened to you? You look absolutely
marvelous.

MARY

Did you say that right?

OSCAR

Apparently not, because I didn't get an answer.

MARY

   (*Adopting a television commercial tone, me-*
   chanically)
Well, you see, I *had* been using an ordinary shampoo, which
left a dull, unattractive film on my hair . . .

OSCAR

Come on, I'm interested. The hair is different—the clothes
—the makeup. Clearly loving hands have been at work.

MARY

   (*Putting her coat and handbag aside and sitting*
   down, tentatively)

23

Yes, but you're not supposed to notice. I mean you're supposed to have an appreciative gleam in your eye, but you don't have to remind me of the dreary hours at Elizabeth Arden's—

OSCAR

Appreciative gleam? I've been casting you lustful glances. You're just too pure to notice. What caused the transformation?

MARY
(*Still not located in space*)
Well, being divorced is like being hit by a Mack truck. If you live through it, you start looking very carefully to the right and to the left. While I was looking I noticed that I was the only twenty-eight-year-old girl wearing a polo coat and no lipstick.

OSCAR

You were? I never noticed.
(*Starting toward kitchen*)
But let me see if I can locate our—

MARY
(*Quickly taking a cigarette from a box on the table*)
No, no—please—wait. Let me have a cigarette first.

OSCAR
(*Lighting it for her*)
You nervous?

24

MARY

Certainly not. But I haven't seen Bob in nine months. I guess I can last another five minutes. Besides, you and I have a lot to talk about. How's Jennifer?

OSCAR

(*Quiet and offhand tone*)
Well, she had this illegitimate baby after she met that man from Gristede's, but it's all right now. . . .

MARY

(*Nodding, looking about the room*)
Oh? Good! And how's everything at the office?

OSCAR

You haven't heard one word I said.

MARY

(*Caught*)
You're right. I'm not listening. And I *am* nervous. I shouldn't have come.

OSCAR

(*Puts his hands on the arm of her chair. Sympathetically*)
Mary, do you still—

MARY

(*Quickly*)
I don't still—anything.

OSCAR

I'm sorry. I should have realized that—

MARY

Stop it. Don't give me that sad spaniel expression, as though you'd just looked at the X rays. I'm all right, Doctor. Just fine.

> (BOB *appears from kitchen, stops short. His words are awkwardly spaced*)

BOB

Well. Hello. You did get here.

OSCAR

Of course, she knew the address.
> (OSCAR *starts toward the office*)

BOB

> (*Not wanting to be left alone*)

Oscar!

> (MARY *gets to her feet, ill at ease*)

OSCAR

Be right back.
> (OSCAR *goes into office, leaving the door open.* MARY *turns toward* BOB *and her nerves now vanish. But* BOB's *are quickly in bad shape*)

MARY

Hello.

Act One

BOB

(*A step to her*)
You look very different. You've changed. I was going to ask
you how you've been. But I can see. You've been fine.

MARY

How about you? Did you ever clear up that case of athlete's
foot?

BOB

(*Almost under his breath*)
No—you haven't changed.

MARY

(*This flusters her briefly. She crosses to the desk,
dips a hand into the bowl of dried apricots*)
Well, you know what they say—the more we change, the more
we stay the same. Good Lord! These are dried apricots.

BOB

What did you think they were?

MARY

Ears.

BOB

(*Ignoring it*)
I want to say that I appreciate your coming. I'm sure you
didn't *want* to.

MARY
(*Circling below the desk toward a plant on a
low bookcase*)
Nonsense. It put my mind at ease. You can't think how often
I've worried about the philodendron.

BOB
(*Picking up tax papers*)
I'm sure. Now, Oscar has explained to you that my—our—
1962 income tax returns are being—

MARY
I advise you to make a clean breast of it. Admit everything.

BOB
This does not happen to be a subject for comedy. I've got to
get this straightened out. I'm getting married in two weeks.

MARY
(*Really stunned*)
Oh?

BOB
I thought you knew. Surely Oscar must have—

MARY
Of course! And it went right out of my head.
(*Sitting near the desk*)
But how nice! Do I know her?

BOB
No, you don't.

Act One

MARY

Do you?

BOB
(*Chooses to ignore this*)

Her name is Tiffany Richards.

MARY

Tiffany. I'll bet she uses brown ink. And when she writes she draws little circles over the *i*'s.

BOB

She is a beautiful, lovely girl with a head on her shoulders.

MARY

How useful!

BOB
(*Spluttering with irritation*)

You really do have a talent for—you've been here five minutes, and already I'm—

MARY
(*With maddening calm*)

Have a dried apricot.

BOB
(*Striding to office door*)

Oscar, have you fallen asleep in there?

OSCAR
(*Off*)

Coming!

29

BOB

> (*Moving away from* MARY *as* OSCAR *appears
> from office*)

Shall we get on with this?

> (*To* MARY)

I know you have to get back to Philadelphia—

MARY

I'm staying in town tonight, so you may consider that my
time is your time.

OSCAR

> (*Sits at the desk, handing* MARY *a batch of can-
> celed checks*)

Okay, Mary, will you look through these checks? Most of
them you've signed.

MARY

Oh, dear—I'm not going to remember *any* of these, Oscar—

OSCAR

It'll come. Just give yourself time. You understand that we're
particularly looking for items that might be deductible. Business entertaining, professional gifts, and so forth.

MARY

> (*Working her way through the checks*)

L. Bernstein—seventy-eight dollars. That's impossible. The
only L. Bernstein I know is Leonard Bernstein and I don't
know Leonard Bernstein.

Act One

OSCAR

(*Pointing it out*)
This is L. Bernstein, D.D.S. A dentist.

BOB

(*Shaking his head*)
I told you—Sidney Bauer is my dentist.

MARY

Dentist, dentist, dentist.
(*Snapping her fingers*)
Listen—it's that man in Boston!

BOB

What man in Boston?

MARY

Don't you remember that crazy restaurant where you go down
all the stairs? And you thought you got a stone in the curry
—but it was your inlay?

BOB

Oh.

MARY

And we drove all the way out to Framingham because he was
the only dentist who'd take you on Sunday?

BOB

Yeah, yeah, yeah.

MARY

By the way, how is that inlay?

BOB

Just grand. How are your crowns?
                (*They turn from each other*)

OSCAR
                (*Stopping this*)
And we have Mrs. Robert Connors—three hundred dollars.

BOB

Mrs. Connors?

MARY

I thought so long as you walked this earth you'd remember
Mrs. Connors. Bootsie Connors and her fish?

BOB

Oh, God. That ghastly weekend in Greenwich.

OSCAR

Okay, tell Daddy.

BOB

Do you remember that young English critic, Irving Mannix?

OSCAR

The angry young man?

BOB

This was two years ago, when he was just a cross young man.

Act One

At that time he was writing long scholarly articles proving that Shakespeare was a homosexual.

MARY

Sort of the intellectual's answer to *Photoplay*.

BOB

Anyway, he was staying here. And we'd been invited to a party at the Connors'.

MARY

So we brought along dear old Irving.

BOB

Do you know the Connors' place in Greenwich?

OSCAR

No.

BOB

Well, the living room is about the size of the ball room at the St. Regis. You feel it would be just the place to sign a treaty.
>   (*As they become interested in the details of the story* BOB *and* MARY *gradually forget their present situation and relax*)

Anyway, it was all too rich for Irving and he started to lap up martinis. In fifteen minutes he was asking our hostess if it was true that the Venetian paneling had been brought over piece by piece from Third Avenue.

OSCAR

Why didn't you take this charmer home?

BOB

Because he passed out. In the library.

MARY

(*It comes back*)
On that damn velvet sofa.

BOB

But he came to just long enough to light a cigarette. Presently the sofa was on fire—really on fire. Our hero jumped up and, with stunning presence of mind, put out the blaze with a tank of tropical fish.

MARY

And these were no run-of-the-bowl goldfish. They came from Haiti and were friends of the family. I mean, they had *names*.

OSCAR

Well, he was a writer. I think we can call that professional entertainment. Okay—we have twenty-five dollars to the Beach Haven Inn.

MARY

That must be yours.

BOB

Nonsense! I was never in . . .
(*And then he remembers*)
The Booksellers—

MARY and BOB

(*Together*)
Convention.

Act One

BOB

That awful hotel with the iron deer in front.

MARY

(*Nodding, her eyes lighting up*)
With the night clerk who looked like Norman Vincent Peale and was so suspicious.

BOB

No wonder he was suspicious!
(*To* OSCAR, *indicating* MARY)
He turns around to get the key and this one says just loud enough for him to hear, "Darling, are we doing the right thing? Maybe we ought to *wait*."

MARY

He was *delighted* to come face to face with sin.

BOB

That's probably why he charged us four bucks to bring up three bottles of beer.

MARY

(*To* OSCAR)
He forgot the bottle opener, and we had to pry them open on the handle of the radiator.

BOB

And one of them was warm or something, so it shot up to the ceiling and all over one of the beds. So we both had to sleep in the other twin bed. . . .
(*His voice has slowed down on this last thought. The remembering is suddenly a bit painful.*

There is a short, awkward silence before MARY
gets to her feet, deliberately breaking the mood)

MARY

Oscar, we're being inefficient. We don't need total recall—
just the facts. I'll take these checks into the office and make
notes on the ones I can remember.

(*Almost before they realize it, she has left them.*
OSCAR *and* BOB *look at one another, then* BOB
looks away)

OSCAR

Mary looks wonderful, don't you think?

BOB

Great.

OSCAR

Like a million bucks.

BOB

(*Nettled*)
I'm afraid the figure that comes into my mind is five thousand
bucks in alimony.

OSCAR

(*Notices* DIRK, *who has just stuck his head in at*
the main door)
Your friend from California.

BOB

(*Relieved at the interruption; his exuberance is*
a bit excessive after the strain with MARY)
Dirk! It's good to see you! How long has it been?

36

Act One

DIRK

I don't know. We were still in sailor suits.

BOB

(*Indicating* OSCAR)

By the way, do you know—

OSCAR

We've met.

BOB

You know, Dirk is the expert we *should* consult!

(*To* DIRK)

You've been married four or five times. How the hell did you manage it?

DIRK

(*Relaxing into a chair*)

I feel like a failure to admit that I was only married three times. Actually, I married my first wife twice—so while there were three marriages, there were just two wives involved.

BOB

Now what? Do you pay both of them alimony?

DIRK

No, my second wife just married a very nice plastic surgeon. He fell in love with her while removing a wart from her shoulder blade. I always thought there was a popular song in that.

BOB

What about your first wife?

37

DIRK

She died.

BOB

See? Them that has, gets!

OSCAR

(*Rises, picks up manuscript from desk, and gives it to* BOB)

I know you two have business to talk about—

(BOB *glances at* DIRK's *manuscript, and his face shows his dismay at having to deal with it*)

—so I'll get back to my arithmetic.

(*He joins* MARY *in the small office, closing the door*)

DIRK

Yes! Down to business.

BOB

(*Avoiding the subject and trying to hold onto his own momentary better spirits*)

Dirk, you look great. Younger than ever. How do you do it?

DIRK

I'll tell you this—it gets harder and harder. If I don't get ten full hours' sleep, they can't do a close-up. If I eat a ham sandwich after four o'clock, it shows on the scale. Ham sandwich, hell. I can gain weight from two Bayer aspirins.

BOB

You sound like the curator of your own museum. Come on, now. It's been worth it, hasn't it?

DIRK

Sure. Except that you develop such nutty habits. Do you know what all middle-aged actors do when they're alone in taxicabs?

BOB

What do they do?
> (DIRK *now demonstrates the business of biting,*
> *open-mouthed, from left to right, to strengthen*
> *the jaw muscles*)

What's that for?

DIRK

It firms up the jawline, old boy. I'll tell you what I dream of doing. My dearest ambition in life is to let my damn jawline go. In fact, that's why I wrote this book.

BOB

> (*Brought back to the subject, embarrassed*)

I see. But—uh—

DIRK

Have you read it?

BOB

Certainly I've read it. Now—the question is, shall I be perfectly frank?
> (DIRK *immediately rises and picks up the manu-*
> *script as if to go*)

You bruise easily. Have you shown this to anybody else?

DIRK

My agent, who thought it was brave, haunting, and hilarious.
I brought it to you first because I knew you.

BOB

I'm sorry, Dirk—but the truth is it's not a book at all. For the
moment we'll rule out the quality of the writing.

DIRK

Let's not rule out anything. What about the quality of the
writing?

BOB

Well, it's—it's—

DIRK

Is "lousy" the word you're groping for?

BOB

Well, let's say it's not prose. Actually, it's not even punctuated. I get the feeling that you waited until you were out of
breath and then threw in a semicolon.

DIRK

Hm.

BOB

However, that could be fixed. What can't be fixed is the con-
tent. It's nothing but anecdotes, really. It's as though you
were just taking up where Louella left off.

DIRK

I gather you do not wish to publish this book. Do you think someone else would take it?

BOB

There are a couple of fringe outfits that I imagine would—

DIRK

I don't want a fringe outfit. Tell me this. How much does it cost to publish a book? Any book?

BOB

It depends on the size of the first printing, the length of the book, the kind of promotion—

DIRK

Let's get down to cases. How much would it cost to bring out my book with a first printing of, say, twelve thousand copies?

BOB

Oh—eight, nine thousand dollars.

DIRK

Let's say I made a check out to you for eighteen thousand dollars. Would you do the book?

BOB

If you proposition women with this same kind of finesse you must get your face slapped a lot.

DIRK

I thought it was worth a try, but don't get mad.

BOB

I'm not mad. I'm surprised. Why does that book mean so much to you? Obviously it isn't the money.

DIRK

It may sound naïve to say it—but being a star has never killed my urge to become an actor. Ten years ago I started to campaign for real parts. But the formula was still making money. So I went right on—passionate kisses and then I'd build the Suez Canal—passionate kisses and then I'd open the golden West—

BOB

What do you figure—you're all through in Hollywood?

DIRK

Technically, no. I have two more pictures to go on my present contract. But when I left, they knew and I knew that I was the sinking ship leaving the rats.

BOB

But why this jump into literature?

DIRK

Well, my press agent thought . . . what the hell, why blame him? *I* thought it might stir up a little interest in me as a man instead of a windup toy. In my fantasies I imagined it would be serialized in *The Saturday Evening Post* with pictures of me looking very seedy. And all of a sudden producers would be saying, "Don't laugh, but do you know who'd be perfect for the degenerate father—Dirk Winston!"

> (MARY *enters from the office, leaving the door open*)

MARY

Bob, I've done my half. Oscar would like to see you.
> (*Seeing* DIRK)

Oh, excuse me.

DIRK

> (*Rising, pleasantly*)

Hello, there.

BOB

This is my—former wife, Mary McKellaway.

MARY

You're Dirk Winston. And your real name is Winston Krib. Dirk is Krib spelled backwards.

DIRK

Good Lord, how did you remember that?

MARY

Oh, I have a head full of the most useless information. I still remember the names of each of the Dionne quintuplets, and the width of the Amazon River.

DIRK

Oh?

MARY

You have no idea how few people care about the width of the Amazon River. I understand you've written a book.

DIRK

That's what I understood, until I talked to Bob here.

MARY

Bob's a special case. He was frightened at an early age by a best seller.

(*She is picking up her coat and handbag*)

DIRK

He was?

BOB

I was not. Why do you say that? It's simply not true. I happen to believe that there's great wisdom in Emerson's remark that you should never read any book until it's a year old. And I'd like to think I'm publishing the kind of books that will be around next year. I'm fed up with novels about tangled lives in Scarsdale—or Old Salem for that matter:

(*Quoting, in a mock literary rhythm*)

"All he knew was that he was a man and she was a woman or had he made some dreadful mistake."

OSCAR

(*Off*)

Bob! Are you coming?

BOB

(*On his way to office*)

Be right back, Dirk.

44

DIRK

Don't think about me. We're all through. I wouldn't want you
to be any clearer.

MARY

Bob, I suppose I might as well go too.

BOB

> (*Turns back to* MARY, *something new on his
> mind*)

Right now?

MARY

Well, don't you have a date?

BOB

I am meeting Tiffany—but couldn't you spare just five minutes? There's something I'd like to ask you.

> (*Assuming her consent,* BOB *goes into the office.*
> MARY *stares after him a moment, absently reach-
> ing for a cigarette. Then she becomes aware of*
> DIRK *again, who has started for the main door
> but is now hesitating, watching her*)

MARY

I used to love your movies. Of course, I didn't see all of them.
My mother wouldn't let me.

DIRK

That's all right. I didn't see all of them, either. My agent
wouldn't let me. Are you a writer?

MARY

No, I work for the *Ladies' Home Journal.* I edit the letters to the editor.

DIRK

You mean they have to be edited?

MARY

(*Nodding*)

It does seem a little like incest, doesn't it?

DIRK

Bob did say you were his *former* wife, didn't he?

MARY

That's right.

DIRK

I'm so glad.

MARY

Why?

DIRK

Because I can ask you to dinner. Will you have dinner with me?

MARY

Tonight?

46

DIRK

You have a date?

MARY

No—no.

DIRK

Then what's wrong with tonight?

MARY

I guess I think we should have known each other longer—like, say, another five minutes.

DIRK

You think you're letting yourself in for an orgy. You think I will ply you with liquor, lure you to my sinful bachelor lodgings, and chase you around the king-size bed.

MARY
(*With a look toward the office*)
Well, I've never been plied with liquor. Maybe I'd like it, but—

DIRK

Come on, we'll have dinner. And *Duck Soup* is playing at the Museum of Modern Art. I promise you I'll be so respectable you'll find me quite tiresome.

MARY
(*On an impulse*)
I have a new dress that would look pretty silly all by itself in Schrafft's. Why not? I'd love to. Do you want to pick me up here? What time?

DIRK

Half an hour?

> (*It occurs to him he'd better check*)

By the way, you don't—live here, do you?

MARY

Oh, no. We're not as civilized as all that. This is business.

DIRK

Fine.

> (*Passing office door*)

See you, Bob. I've got a call in to the Coast.

> (*On his way to the main door, turning back to*
> MARY)

Half an hour?

> (MARY *nods, smiling.* DIRK *goes, closing the
> door.* MARY *turns, a little unsure of herself, sees
> the galleys on the sofa table, abstractedly picks
> them up, and puts her cigarette on an ash tray on
> the table. At almost the same time,* BOB *ap-
> pears from the office, as though in response to*
> DIRK's *farewell, then realizes he is alone with*
> MARY)

BOB

Oh. Mary—thanks for waiting—I—

MARY

> (*She has been aware of his return, but has not
> looked at him. Now she deliberately reads from
> the galleys, in a somewhat questioning voice*)

"He was alone in the middle of the field. He was grateful

Act One

once again to be in possession of his own body. The Queen Anne's lace waved in the breeze like a thousand tiny handkerchiefs . . ."
      (Looks up)
This sounds suspiciously like our friend O'Brynner.
      (Glancing at the first page of the galleys)
And no wonder! I thought you weren't going to do this one.

BOB

Why?

MARY

Because this man writes like a sick elf.

BOB
      (Wanting to brush the matter aside before he is irritated again)
Let's skip that.
      (In a hesitant, slightly strained voice)
Mary—

MARY
      (Adopting his tone)
Bob—

BOB

I've been thinking.
      (Starts to sit on the ottoman)

MARY

I thought you had an odd expression.

49

BOB

(*Jumping up again, a sudden, desperate explosion*)

Could you—would it be absolutely impossible for you to listen to me for three minutes without making one single wisecrack?

MARY

(*Stung—but concealing it*)

I could try.

BOB

(*Earnestly*)

I wish you would. I really wish you would. There is something I want to ask you and I can't do it through a barrage of flippantries.

MARY

You'd be surprised. I don't feel flippant at all. What is it you want to ask me?

BOB

(*Sitting*)

You—know I'm getting married again.

MARY

Yes, I know that.

BOB

Well, I find myself stewing over a very curious thing Tiffany said today.

MARY

Oh?

BOB

Her idea was that people go right on making the same mistakes. I had an eerie feeling that there was something true about that.

(*Realizing that he is groping*)

What I'm trying to say is that I have by God got to make a better job of it this time.

(MARY *turns her head away.* BOB *leans toward her*)

Yes?

MARY

I didn't say anything.

BOB

But you were thinking—

MARY

(*Turns back to him sharply*)

Look, you say your lines, I'll say my lines. You're hoping for better luck this time. *I* hope you'll have better luck this time. Beyond that, I don't see—

BOB

You could tell me what *I* did wrong. When we broke up, I spent many drunken hours thinking how it was all your fault.

(MARY *starts to speak*)

Yes, I know I'm painting a charming portrait of myself—Bob McKellaway as a slob and sorehead. But that's how I felt.

MARY

And that's how you still feel.

BOB

No, by the time I calmed down and cleared the last of your bobby pins out of the bathroom, I realized that half the trouble had to be me.

MARY

You think it can be divided into two equal parts—like a sandwich?

BOB

I think success has no rules, but you can learn a great deal from failure.

MARY

I see. And what you're really looking for is the formula for instant marriage.

BOB

No, I'm not as sappy as that. I'm prepared to make a number of different mistakes this time. I would like not to make the same ones. And I would like some advice.

MARY

Had you thought of writing to Dear Abby?
(*He rises and moves away. She is immediately penitent*)
Bob, I'm sorry for that. That's the kind of thing I promised not to say.
(BOB *returns to her, hopefully*)
But what you're asking is impossible. I can't give you a report card. Is he punctual? Does he complete the task assigned? But you know what? This is so like you. This determination to be sensible in a situation where it isn't sensible to be sensible.

52

Act One

You want to analyze, analyze. Like those people who take an overdose of sleeping pills, and sit there making notes while they're dying. "Four A.M. Vision beginning to blur." You'd do that. You would.

BOB

Maybe.

MARY

What shall I say? That you used to leave your ties on the coffee table? And you always grabbed *The New Yorker* first and took it to the bathroom? And you never talked to me in cars?

BOB

Of course I talked in cars.

MARY

Yes, to the traffic signals. "Come on, dammit, turn green."

BOB

I concentrate when I drive.

MARY

And you were always asking solemn, editorial-type questions beginning Don't You Ever. Don't You Ever order lunch meat? Don't You Ever put the lid back on the mayonnaise? Don't You Ever put your cigarettes out?

BOB

(*Brandishing* MARY's *still-smoking cigarette and putting it out with great vigor*)
Because you never in your life put a cigarette out!

53

MARY

And you always, always put the ice-cube trays back without filling them.

BOB

(*Gesturing toward the kitchen*)
Ice-cube trays? Is that all you remember?

MARY

Aren't you forgetting one small detail? You're the one who walked out.

BOB

Technically, I suppose that's true.

MARY

Technically? There was nothing technical about it. You got up in the middle of the night and slammed out of here. And you know what? I never knew why.

BOB

Like hell you didn't.

MARY

All I knew was, one moment you were in bed, and the next minute you were banging drawers and dumping shirts into a suitcase.

BOB

And that's *all* you remember?
(*Coming nearer*)

Act One

Let me reconstruct the scene for you. You were in bed reading *McCall's*. I was in the bathroom brushing my teeth. Then I put the lights out, came to bed, put my arms around you, and you said, "Okay, let's get those colored lights going."

MARY

I said that?

BOB

I wouldn't be capable of inventing it.

MARY

And was that so terrible?

BOB

Maybe not. But let us say that it had the effect of a cold shower when I wasn't in the mood for a cold shower.

MARY

I see.

BOB

I grant you it was a very small straw to be the last straw. Another time it would have bounced off me. But it had been such a stinker of a day. We got bad notices on the Caine book. The deal for the serial rights fell through. Oh, the usual. Except that I felt a peculiar need for some warmth. I guess I felt I needed a wife.

MARY

(*Hotly*)

I think I was wifely—a lot.

BOB

Sure. On and off. Between jokes.

> (MARY *grabs a sofa pillow as though she were going to hit him with it, but is deflected by* OSCAR's *return from the office. He sees what she is doing*)

OSCAR

Please don't be embarrassed on my account. I'm delighted. I hate a friendly divorce. A lawyer is never entirely comfortable with a friendly divorce, any more than a good mortician wants to finish his job and then have the patient sit up on the table.

> (MARY, *without saying a word, picks up her coat, her suitcase, gloves, and handbag and leaves by the main door.* OSCAR *looks at* BOB)

Did you read Walter Lippmann today? I thought it was an awfully good piece.

BOB

Oscar, don't be urbane all the time. I can't stand it.

> (*Fuming*)

You see why I didn't want to see her again? When you said she was coming, I should have walked out that front door! I don't understand it. I thought she had lost the power to enrage me. Maybe I took the bandages off too soon. Maybe I—

> (*Stops as he sees* MARY *returning with her suitcase*)

Did you forget something?

MARY

No, dammit, I *remembered* something. Having made my dramatic exit, I realized that this is where I'm being picked up. I *have* to stay here for another ten minutes.

BOB

I see.

MARY

And furthermore, I will have to use your room to change in.
(*To* OSCAR)
Oscar, if the phone rings, it may be for me. Will *you* take it?
The Algonquin is supposed to call and confirm my room for
tonight.

BOB

There's a new telephone in the . . .
(MARY *goes off to the bedroom, not exactly
slamming the door but letting it close pretty ar-
rogantly behind her.* BOB *starts to follow but is
stopped by* OSCAR)

OSCAR

Never mind her. We have something more important to talk
about.
(*Sitting at the desk*)
I have been over all the figures and am now ready to give my
state of the Union address.

BOB

(*Trying to tear his mind away from* MARY, *but
still edgy and upset*)
First, tell me about that tax thing.

OSCAR

Oh, my guess is that we'll get it down somewhere in the
neighborhood of eighteen hundred, two thousand dollars.

BOB

That would be more like it.

OSCAR

You said you wanted my advice on the over-all picture. Let me ask you a couple of questions. Tiffany comes from a wealthy family, doesn't she?

BOB

What has that got to do with anything?

OSCAR

A lot. She has to be supported. You can't support her. I have now been through what we shall laughingly call your books, and you're not supporting yourself.

BOB

You're joking.

OSCAR

Then why aren't you laughing?

BOB

Look. If you're trying in some left-handed way to tell me I can't get married, you're wasting your breath. I'm thirty-six years old, and this is a—

OSCAR

Free country? Don't you believe it. People pick up the most erroneous ideas from popular songs. Let me tell you something. If all you've got is the sun in the morning and the moon at night, you're in trouble.

Act One

BOB

What are you talking about? I take eighteen thousand a year
out of the company—plus bonuses.

OSCAR

That's right.

BOB

That may be cigarette money to the Rockefellers, but it still
feels like a lot to me. Hell, my father never made more than
five thousand a year in his life and he put four boys through
college.

OSCAR

Let's not dwell on the glories of the past. *I* have the figures for
this year. Do you want to hear them?

BOB

No.
(*Starts for bedroom and stops*)
Oh, yes, I suppose so.

OSCAR
(*Referring to a work sheet*)
We start with your base salary—eighteen thousand—plus one
thousand dollars sales bonus. By the way, that was down from
preceding years.

BOB

Sales were down.

OSCAR

So that's nineteen thousand dollars. Against that, we have:
thirty-two hundred, rent; two thousand, eighty, maid service;

59

four thousand, nine hundred, food and liquor; five thousand, alimony to Mary—

                              BOB

And that's ridiculous.
          (*Shouting at the bedroom door*)
She's working.

                              OSCAR

That was the decision of the court. You can't do anything about it.
          (*Picking up where he left off*)
Five thousand to Mary. Six hundred and eighty, club dues and entertainment. Six hundred, clothes. Nine hundred, books, furnishings, dry cleaning. Eleven hundred, insurance and medical. Twenty-seven hundred, taxes. We now have a total of twenty-one thousand, one hundred and sixty dollars. You do have three thousand in available savings, but most of that will go for that old tax bill.

                              BOB

Here, let me see that thing.
          (*Takes work sheet from* OSCAR)

                              OSCAR

You can juggle those figures any way you want to. But you're not going to change the fact that you are already spending twenty-one thousand on an income of nineteen. It's not just that you can't support another wife. You'd be ill-advised to buy a canary.

                              BOB

It can't be as complicated as you're pretending—

OSCAR

Actually, it's even more complicated. You must keep in mind that if you ever wanted to divorce Tiffany, you'd be in a hopeless position, financially.

BOB

(*Outburst*)
I'm not going to divorce Tiffany! Why would I divorce Tiffany?

OSCAR

Your attitude does you credit.

BOB

Here. Some of these expenses I can cut.

OSCAR

Yes, you could move to a cheaper apartment. You don't have to belong to the New York Athletic Club. You might save seven or eight hundred dollars. However, I have met Tiffany. I doubt that you could keep her in cashmere sweaters for that. She doesn't work, does she?

BOB

Oh, she does volunteer things.

OSCAR

Maybe her father would give her an allowance.

BOB

Maybe we could take in boarders. Any more bright ideas? What the hell am I supposed to do? Stay single for the rest of my life and sleep around? Or do I remain celibate and take cold showers and get plenty of exercise?

OSCAR

Fortunately, you belong to the Athletic Club.
> (*Telephone rings.* OSCAR *answers it*)

Hello. That's right. Can I take the message?
> (MARY, *in dressing gown, pokes her head out of the bedroom door*)

I see. Will you wait one minute?
> (*To* MARY)

They haven't got a single but they can give you a suite!

MARY

Tell them never mind. I'm not paying twenty-four dollars for one night. I'll go to the Biltmore.

BOB

> (*Not graciously, just realistically*)

If you want to, you can stay here. I'm going to be in Goshen for the weekend.

MARY

Stay here?

BOB

I won't be here. You'll be perfectly safe.

MARY

I'm not worried. I was perfectly safe when you *were* here.
> (MARY *disappears, shutting the door again*)

BOB

I shouldn't have divorced her. I should have shot her.

Act One

OSCAR

    (*Into phone*)
Thank you, she'll make other arrangements.
    (*Doorbell, as* OSCAR *hangs up*)

BOB

    (*Going to the front door*)
With my luck, this'll be a telegram saying that my rich old uncle died and left his money to a kindly waitress.
    (BOB *opens the door to* DIRK, *and is surprised to see him*)
Oh. Hello again.

DIRK

Hello. Is she ready?

BOB

Who?

DIRK

Do I get a choice? I'm calling for Mary.

BOB

For Mary? For what?

DIRK

For dinner. Isn't that all right? Should my mother have called your mother?

BOB

Don't be ridiculous. I just didn't know, that's all.

63

OSCAR

You see, Bob thinks when he brings a book back to the library, it'll never go out again.

BOB

Bob doesn't think anything. I had always supposed that Mr. Winston only went out with women whose names ended in *a*. Like Lana. Or Ava. And I'm a little puzzled as to why he wants to take my ex-wife to dinner.

DIRK

Because she looked hungry. You damn fool! Because she strikes me as an exceptionally attractive girl.

BOB

And you would know.

DIRK

That's right. I don't want to pull rank or anything—but I think it might be fair to assume I know at least as much about women as you do about books. Perhaps more.

BOB

Look, you misunderstand me. I am delighted that you find my former wife attractive. I'm charmed that you are taking her out. If you decide to marry her, I'll send up rockets. In fact, you can count on me as your best man.

OSCAR

Marry her and you count on him as your publisher.

Act One

BOB

(*Overheated*)

Absolutely! Now, there's a brilliant idea! Why didn't I think of it? Oscar's got a head on both his shoulders. I could solve your problems, you could solve my problems.

DIRK

You've got to be joking.

BOB

(*Lying back on the sofa and kicking off his loafers*)

Why? This is the age of the deal! You scratch me and I'll scratch you! Don't you read the papers? Why should I be out of touch?

OSCAR

Bob—

DIRK

No, let's listen to him. I couldn't be more impressed. It stirs memories of the past—I keep thinking, "Louis B. Mayer, thou shouldst be living at this hour!"

BOB

(*To* OSCAR)

See? You're shocked. But he's been around!

DIRK

And back. It couldn't be more reasonable. He has an unmarketable wife and I have an unmarketable book. He thinks we should pool our lack of resources. I haven't had such a fascinating offer in years.

65

(The bedroom door opens and MARY *appears, beautiful in a low-cut dress)*

MARY

Hello! I think I'm all collected.
　　(All rise)

　　(She senses the tension in the air)
What are you all staring at? Is something showing?

DIRK

Yes, and it looks delicious. Are we ready?
　　(He gets MARY's *coat as* MARY *goes to* OSCAR *and kisses him)*

MARY

　　(To BOB)
I suppose it's all right if I pick up that bag later tonight?

BOB

Certainly. But how will you get in?

MARY

　　(Waving a bunch of keys from out of her handbag)
I still have my keys. Have you been missing things?

DIRK

Shall we run along? I double-parked down there.

MARY

　　(Breezing through doorway, calling back to OS-CAR *and* BOB)
Good night!

66

Act One

                    BOB and OSCAR
          (*She's already gone*)
Good night.

                         DIRK
          (*Ready to go, turning back to* BOB *from the door-
          way, grinning*)
I think you've got yourself a deal.
          (DIRK *goes, closing door behind him.* BOB *heaves
          a great sigh of exasperation and snatches up the
          galleys*)

                        OSCAR
          (*After watching* BOB *for a moment*)
I've known you for twenty years and I never realized you had
this flair for comedy.
          (*No answer from* BOB, *trying to concentrate on
          galleys*)
You *were* joking?

                         BOB
          (*Crossly*)
Of course I was joking.
          (*Looking up as the thought crosses his mind*)
But wouldn't I like to see him try! It'd be an education for
him.
          (OSCAR *pokes the work sheet under his nose*)
Don't, don't, don't. I don't want to hear another word about
my untidy affairs.
          (*Turns his attention to galleys again*)

                          67

OSCAR
(Following BOB *to the desk)*
What's the matter with you?

BOB
(Sharply, not lyrically, and without looking up)
Say I'm weary, say I'm sad, say that health and wealth have missed me, and you've said it.
*(*BOB *is now rapidly crossing out great sections of the galleys)*

OSCAR
Why are you *slashing* at those galleys?

BOB
Because this man writes like a sick elf!
(And BOB *is going at it with renewed vigor as the* CURTAIN FALLS*)*

END OF ACT ONE

Act Two

The moment the curtain is up, DIRK and MARY enter by the main door, stomping their feet and brushing snow from their clothes. It is shortly after midnight and the room is dark except for the glow from the window. MARY turns on the hall light just inside the front door.

DIRK

Did you get wet?

MARY

No, except for my hair.

DIRK

It doesn't look wet.

MARY

No, but you watch. In five minutes it'll be so fuzzy I'll be able to cut a piece off and clean my suede shoes.

DIRK

Would you feel safer if I left the door open?

69

MARY

Oh dear! I felt perfectly safe until you asked that question.

DIRK

The question is withdrawn.

MARY

Isn't this the silliest snowstorm?
> (*Going to the window, looking out*)

DIRK

> (*Closing the door and following her*)

I come from California. I think it's a lovely snowstorm.

MARY

But those great big flakes swirling around! It looks so phoney. Like—do you remember those big glass paperweights and you turned them upside down and it snowed? That's how it looks.
> (*Turns and is surprised to find him right behind her. Unsettled, she points to her bag near the bedroom door*)

Here's that damn bag. Remember—you're not coming back out with me. I'll get a cab.

DIRK

In *this*? You'd never. And here I am—ready—willing—cheaper.

MARY

If I had a brain in my head, I'd have taken it with me and we could have dropped it off at the Biltmore.
> (MARY *is holding the suitcase in her hand. As* DIRK *goes to take it from her, his hand rests on hers a moment*)

Act Two

DIRK

Does everybody tell you how pretty you are?

MARY
(*Takes her hand away—flustered*)
Oh, you *are* a good actor! You could play anything.
(*Changing the subject*)
You know what? It's really idiotic, our going back out in that blizzard. We're not delivering the serum.
(*She comes into the room and turns on a lamp*)
Why don't I just *stay* here?
(Dirk *puts the bag down and looks toward the bedroom. In answer to his unspoken question*)
Oh, he's safely in Goshen with a beautiful, lovely girl with a head on her shoulders.
(*She has remembered* Bob's *description word for word.* Dirk *stares at her a second, then heads for the bar table*)

DIRK

Do you suppose we can have a drink, or did Bob get the custody of the liquor?

MARY

(*She is already a couple of cocktails in, and is beginning to like it*)
Sure, let's have a drink. But make mine light. I'm beginning to feel that champagne.
(*She turns on another lamp*)
Do you realize we were three hours in that restaurant? That's the nice thing about having dinner with somebody you're not married to.

71

(She starts to sit on the sofa, then after a glance at DIRK, who is making the drinks, discreetly chooses a chair)
You have so much more to talk about.

DIRK

All I found out about you is that you're allergic to penicillin and you love *The Catcher in the Rye.*

MARY

That's all? That's a lot. I want to hear about you. Are you going to get your book published?

DIRK

I am going to make every possible effort.
(Hands her a drink)
That's mostly water.
(He moves a chair close to her and sits)
You and Bob must have spent a lot of time with authors. What do *they* talk about?

MARY

You don't think they talk about *books?* They talk about first serial rights, second serial rights, movie rights, and how they're going to form a corporation to publish their next one so they can call it a capital gain and move to Jamaica.

DIRK

They sound just like actors.

MARY

It's terrible when you feel a writer is trying out his material on you. You never know exactly what reaction they expect, but you have to keep looking so *interested* your eyebrows get tired.

> (*She has made a concentrated face to show what she means.* DIRK *grins*),

DIRK

I know a guy who used to work with Disney. He'd actually tell you the whole plot of an animated cartoon—frame by frame. But he was a classic case. He could bore the birds back onto the trees. He never stopped talking—never. If he took a drink, he'd hold his hand up—

> (*He demonstrates this*)

—so you couldn't put a word in until he was back with you.

> (MARY *laughs at the demonstration, then calms down into a small silence, which* DIRK *fills*)

Your eyes are so blue—and so liquid. I feel they might spill right down your cheeks.

MARY

> (*Quick with the answer, moving away to get a cigarette, leaving her drink behind*)

That's because I need glasses and won't wear them.

DIRK

> (*Curious and interested*)

Why do you do that?

MARY

Do what?

DIRK

You jump when you get a compliment.

MARY
                    (*Too quickly*)
No, I don't.

DIRK
You're actually embarrassed.

MARY
                    (A *shade defensively, lighting her cigarette*)
Why should I be embarrassed?

DIRK
I don't know. But you are. You come bustling in to change
the subject, like a nervous hostess who's discovered that two
of the guests are quarreling.
                    (*Imitating the hostess*)
"Now, come along, Harry—there's somebody very nice I want
you to meet."

MARY
                    (*Sits at one end of sofa*)
All right. Pay me pretty compliments and I won't change the
subject.

DIRK
And you won't make jokes?
                    (MARY *is stunned by the echo of* BOB's *remark*)

MARY
What? What?

DIRK
Shouldn't I have said that?

74

Act Two

MARY

No, that's all right. It's been said before. Just recently, in fact. I suppose I should take a course and find out what a girl should answer when a gentleman says "Tell me, pretty maiden, are there any more at home like you?" Though it would hardly pay. It doesn't come up that often.

DIRK

I thought little girls learned things like that when they were three years old.
          (*He moves nearer to her, bringing her drink*)

MARY

Oh, but I'm a very retarded case. It's only just this year I learned how to put my hair up in rollers.

DIRK

What did you do before that?

MARY

I wore it pinned back in a bun. And when it had to be cut, *I* cut it, or I went somewhere and *they* cut it. Lately I've been going to Elizabeth Arden, and I want you to know that it's a whole new way of life.

DIRK

So I'm told.

MARY

At Arden's they don't just cut your hair—never. They *shape* it. And they honestly think a good shaping is as important as a cure for cancer. The hairdresser really blanched when he saw my bun. I could hear him thinking, "Thank God she came to me—another month and it might have been too late."

DIRK

Well, I think your hair looks lovely. Now say thank you.

MARY

Thank you.

DIRK

See how easy it is?

MARY
(*Jumping up, self-conscious*)
I—Oh—Tell me about your book.
(*Picks up the manuscript*)

DIRK
(*Taking the manuscript from* MARY)
What can I tell you? It weighs three quarters of a pound. It takes eighty-four cents in stamps to mail it.
(*Tosses it on sofa table and goes to the bar for another drink*)

MARY

Don't talk like that. You mustn't lose faith in it just because Bob didn't like it. Bob's a good publisher but he makes mistakes. Did you have any help with this book?

DIRK

You mean, did I *tell* it to somebody? No.

76

Act Two

MARY

I'm glad. All these "as told to" books have such a spooky flavor about them. First the personality is all drained off. Then, to compensate, something else is pumped in—sex or religion or Scott Fitzgerald. I fully expect that any day now we're going to have The Confessions of Saint Augustine—as told to Gerold Frank.

DIRK
(Returning to her)

Mary—

MARY

What?

DIRK

You just said Bob makes mistakes. But how did he ever let you slip through his fingers?

MARY

Just lucky, I guess.

DIRK

I think I am beginning to see the clue to this little puzzle.

MARY

What puzzle?

DIRK

You.

MARY

I'd love to think I was a puzzle. A woman of mystery. Smiling and enigmatic on the surface—but underneath, a tigress.

77

(*Change of mood, straightforward*)
I hate to admit it, but what you see is all there is. Underneath this plain, girlish exterior, there's a very plain girl.

Ah, but what happened to make you *decide* it was such a plain exterior? It was the divorce, wasn't it? It was Bob.

MARY

Bob? I decided *that* when I was thirteen years old. We can't blame Bob for everything.

DIRK

At thirteen, all by yourself, you decided that?

MARY
(*Sitting on the ottoman*)
Oh, there were people around, but I can't say they gave me any argument. Do you ever look at little girls?

DIRK

How little?

MARY
(*Rather intensely, as she remembers and thinks about it. The intensity is perhaps increased by the amount she's had to drink*)
You take two little girls. One of them is pink and round, with curly hair and yards of eyelashes. The other one is pale and bony, with thin, wispy hair and two little ears poking through —like the handles on a sugar bowl. Okay, which one of these little girls is going to have to wear braces on her teeth?

Act Two

DIRK

The wispy one.

MARY
(*As though awarding him a prize*)
You've got it.
                (*Seeing herself again, taking a sip of her drink*)
That was me. Braces on my teeth, Band-Aids on my knees,
freckles on my nose. All elbows and shoulder blades. For two
years running I got picked to play the consumptive orphan in
Michael O'Halloran.

DIRK

That was talent.

MARY

That was typecasting.

DIRK

All adolescents go through something. I had the worst case
of acne in the history of the world. For three years I was a
Technicolor marvel. You wouldn't remember when Fleisch-
mann's Yeast was the big thing. I used to eat Fleischmann's
Yeast and drink water until I couldn't move without gurgling.
I imagine I was actually fermenting.

MARY

I never ate yeast, but once I sent away secretly for Stillman's
freckle cream. I guess I used too much, because I just peeled
and peeled. I had to pretend it was a sunburn.

79

DIRK

I used to pretend I hated everybody. Especially girls, because I was too self-conscious to talk to them.

MARY

You made a spectacular recovery.

DIRK

I may even have overdone it. But why didn't you—

MARY

Make a recovery? Well, it was sort of different with me. When I was a kid, I mean really a kid, I never worried about the way I looked, because I thought—I *knew*—I'd grow up to be beautiful just like my sister Clara.

DIRK

Was she so beautiful?

MARY

Clara? She had bright red hair and brown eyes and she always had a faintly startled look, as if she'd just come out of a dark theater into the sunlight. People who met her would be so busy staring they'd forget to finish their sentences.

DIRK

I can see that would have been something of a cross for you.

MARY

No, I thought it was insurance. Clara was six years older than I was, and I thought "I'll grow up to look just like that." One day I was measuring myself—I was about fourteen—and I realized I hadn't grown at all, not an inch, in a whole year.

Act Two

And then it came to me. I wasn't going to grow any more. I was *up*. And I didn't look anything at all like Clara.

DIRK

And you weren't satisfied to look like Mary?

MARY

I certainly was not. I went rushing to my father, and I asked him when I was going to look like Clara. Poor man. He didn't know what to say.

DIRK

What did he say?

MARY

He said "Darling, we wouldn't want two Claras. You're the bright one." That did it. I could have faced being plain, but to be plain *and* bright! In the high school I went to, that was a beatable combination.

DIRK

So you decided to get on the debating team.

MARY

How did you know?

DIRK

Girls who feel they are not going to be invited to dances always get on the debating team.

MARY

And I worked on the school newspaper. And I imagined all the time that I was really Catherine Earnshaw.

DIRK

Catherine who?

MARY

The girl in *Wuthering Heights*. Cathy.

DIRK

Oh, Merle Oberon.

MARY

That's right. I used to dream that somewhere there was a strange, dark man whose heart was quietly breaking for me. On rainy nights I'd open the window and imagine I could hear him calling—"Oh, my wild, sweet Cathy!" The colds I got! And of course the only dark man I ever saw was the middle-aged dentist who used to adjust the braces on my teeth.

DIRK

And you're still cross about it.

MARY

Is that how I sound? I don't feel that way. I feel wistful. I think of that sappy little girl and I wonder what happened to her.

DIRK

Nothing happened. She hasn't changed at all.

MARY

You mean I haven't changed at all? That's a hell of a thing to say.

Act Two

DIRK

Oh, I'm certain you've changed in appearance. That's clear enough. But you yourself haven't changed. Somewhere inside you, you're *still* wearing braces on your teeth.

MARY

Oh, come, come. I came to the big city. I learned to tip waiters. I read *The New Yorker.* I got married.

DIRK

And nothing took. Do you know what's strange?

MARY

What?

DIRK

Here you are—so lovely. And nobody falls in love with you.

MARY

Oh, is that so? And where did you get that idea?

DIRK

From you.

MARY

You're crazy. I never said—listen, lots of people—well, Bob certainly was in love with me—

DIRK

You really thought so?

83

MARY

Of course! Why else would he marry me? There was no dowry, or anything.

DIRK

I don't know. Why did he?

MARY

(*Seriously unsettled beneath her insistent assurance*)
Because he felt that—because we both—listen, what is this?
(*Rises*)
I haven't answered so many idiotic questions since I tried to open a charge account at Saks!
(*Moves away to the fireplace*)
There must be a genteel, ladylike way of telling you that it's none of your damn business!

DIRK

I knew I'd get a rise out of you when I said that about Bob.

MARY

Then why did you say it?

DIRK

Of course Bob was in love with you. But you don't believe it. You never believed it.

MARY

(*Turns to him, alert*)
What did he tell you?

84

DIRK

Nothing. You're the evidence. Women who believe they're attractive have a certain air about them. You don't. Your reflexes are off.

MARY
(*Now furious*)
I will match my reflexes with your manners any old day! And now, unless you have some other little speech all rehearsed, I suggest you go upstairs or downstairs or wherever it is you call home!

DIRK

Now you're mad.

MARY

Oh, you *are* the quick one! Nothing is wasted on you. Of course I'm mad! What did you expect I'd be?

DIRK

I didn't know. I never met anybody quite like you before.

MARY

We're even. I never met anybody like you, either.
(*Sitting at one end of the sofa*)
Which doesn't explain why I let myself be taken in by that richer, milder, longer-lasting M-G-M charm.

DIRK

Oh, *were* you—taken in?

MARY

I must have been. Why else would I sit here—babbling like an idiot, pouring out my little girlish secrets! That's not part of my regular act. I don't learn.
(DIRK *sits near* MARY *on sofa*)
I guess I never will learn.

DIRK

(*Putting his hands on her shoulders and speaking earnestly and directly*)
Mary, do you know what I feel? I feel—

MARY

(*Coolly, sarcastically*)
You feel as though you were seeing me—for the first time.

DIRK

I'll tell you something you ought to learn. You really ought to learn when to shut up.
(*With real dispatch, he takes her into his arms and kisses her firmly.* MARY *is too startled at first to protest, and later she is maybe too interested. When they break off,* DIRK *puts one finger gently to her lips*)
Shh! Now once more—quickly, before you lose your nerve.
(*He kisses her again*)

MARY

(*Finally*)
I feel dizzy.

DIRK

That's suitable.

86

Left to Right: MICHAEL RENNIE as Dirk Winston, BARBARA
BEL GEDDES as Mary McKellaway, BARRY NELSON as Bob
McKellaway.

Left to Right: BARBARA BEL GEDDES as Mary and BARRY NELSON as Bob McKellaway

Left to Right: JOHN CROMWELL as Oscar Nelson, BARBARA BEL GEDDES as Mary McKellaway, BARRY NELSON as Bob McKellaway.

Left to Right: BARRY NELSON as Bob McKellaway and BETSY
VON FURSTENBERG as Tiffany Richards.

MARY

It's just that I haven't kissed anybody, lately. But it's like riding a bicycle. It does come back to you.

DIRK

And you don't even have to worry about the calories.

MARY

You know—you're very nice. And about ninety-five per cent correct.

DIRK

About what?

MARY

About a lot of things. But why are you bothering with me?

DIRK

I'm being bribed.

MARY
(*Taking it as a joke, of course*)
I *knew* that. But there must be other reasons. I like *you* because you hurt my feelings and made me lose my temper.

DIRK

And that's a reason?

MARY

To me it is. I've gone so long not reacting to anything, it seems somehow reassuring. It's like—well—if you were absolutely convinced that you had no feeling in your hand, you'd be relieved to burn your fingers.

DIRK

(*Picking up her hand and kissing it*)

What can we do for those fingers? I like you because I think that, with any encouragement, I might fall in love with you.

(*She is silent*)

If you're going to say anything, say what you're thinking. Don't invent something.

MARY

(*Facing up to this*)

I'm thinking I'd really like to believe that. So I will.

DIRK

That's my girl.

> (*And he is kissing her again as* BOB *enters.* BOB, *too, is snowy as he comes in the main door. He stops dead at what he sees*)

BOB

Mary. What are *you* doing here?

DIRK

Don't ask rhetorical questions. Surely you can see what she's doing.

BOB

> (*Embarrassed, bothered by some instinctive reaction he doesn't understand, and trying to be cordial. After all, it's what he hoped for. His reactions are actually disturbingly mixed*)

All I meant, really, was to indicate my surprise that Mary was

88

here. I thought we left it that she was going to the Biltmore. I mean—what *is* the situation now?
>(*To* MARY, *and still floundering*)

I mean, are you just coming or going?

MARY
>(*Sweetly. She's a little bit high*)

I'm staying. What about you?

DIRK

We thought you were on your way to Goshen.

BOB
>(*Taking off his coat*)

I *was* on my way to Goshen, but there's a blizzard out there. We couldn't even get on the thruway.

MARY

And I wasn't privy to your change of plans.
>(*Turns to* DIRK)

Do you know I never in my whole life used the word privy before?

DIRK

Not even for—?

MARY
>(*Shaking her head rapidly*)

Nope, never. Don't you hate places where they have cute names for the men's room?

DIRK

I hate places where they have cute names for the places. Did you ever hear of a nightclub called the Chez When?

(BOB *moves toward the desk aimlessly. They are continuing their conversation as though he hadn't come in*)

MARY

(*Eyes widening*)

No.

DIRK

What do you call it when the words are accidentally twisted? Where the minister says the Lord is a shoving leopard—?

MARY

I think that's a spoonerism. I'm always getting words twisted like that. I was buying a hammock for the porch at home. And in a crowded elevator I said, "Miss, where do you have perch forniture?"

DIRK

Perch forniture?

MARY

Don't you just know the unsuitable things that would go on in perch forniture?

(*As they laugh, they become more aware of* BOB, *who is feeling very much like a fifth wheel and not liking it*)

DIRK

Bob, why don't you get yourself a drink?

BOB

Thank you. You're the soul of hospitality.

(*He does go to get himself a drink*)

Act Two

DIRK

Well . . .

MARY

Pay no attention to Bob. It's just that he's systematic. He has his day all planned out. He makes a list. And the snow wasn't on his list and you weren't on his list.

DIRK
(*A sly look at* BOB)
But we had such an interesting chat at six o'clock. I thought I was definitely in his plans—on his list.

BOB

I'm sorry if I sounded rude. But it happens to be one-thirty, and any hour now I'd like to know where I'm going to lay my head.
(*To* MARY)
Did I understand you to say you were staying here?

MARY
(*Giddily*)
Yes. I'm sleepy. I do not wish to go out into the night that covers me black as the pit from pole to pole. Remember, women and children first. That's the law of the sea. And I'm sure it goes for snowstorms.

BOB

Naturally I don't expect you to go out in this.
(*Unable to restrain a note of irony*)
Would it be all right if I slept here on the couch?

MARY

Certainly. Be your guest.

DIRK

(*To* MARY)
Our host is beginning to look glassy-eyed. And since we seem
to be sitting on his final resting place, I'd better leave.
(*Rising*)
But it was a lovely evening.
(*Takes* MARY's *hand*)

MARY

(*Rising with* DIRK)
I thought so. I really thought so.
(*They go hand in hand toward the door.* DIRK
gets his coat)

DIRK

I'll call you first thing in the morning. Is ten o'clock too early?

MARY

Ten o'clock is fine.
(DIRK *kisses her lightly but definitely*)

DIRK

(*To* MARY)
Good night—
(*To* BOB, *cheerily*)
Good night!

BOB

Night.
(DIRK *goes, closing the main door behind him*)

(*There is a slight moment of awkwardness, then*

Act Two

> Bob *goes toward the closet*)

Well, I'll get myself a blanket and some sheets. I imagine
that extra blanket is still in the storage closet.

MARY

> (*Hasn't stirred*)

I imagine.

BOB

> (*Having got out a sheet and blanket*)

Too bad we can't open the window. This place is full of
smoke.

> (*Waving his arms about to dispel imaginary
> smoke*)

MARY

Uh-hm.

BOB

> (*Picks up a large ash tray from the coffee table
> and dumps the contents of the sofa table ash tray
> and the mantel ash tray into it. Then empties
> the large one into the fireplace. Finally, he speaks
> his mind*)

I must say that I'm rather surprised at you.

MARY

> (*Bright, cheery*)

Yes. I'm a little surprised at me, too.

BOB

You've been drinking.

MARY
(*Airily*)
Yep, that's exactly what I've been doing. It's taught me a valuable lesson. You know what's the matter with this country? Too much sobriety. Too many sober persons.

BOB
May I suggest that you get yourself to bed before you pass right out?

MARY
No, you may not suggest one thing. I do not require your solasitude.

BOB
Solasitude? Solicitude!

MARY
(*Pleasantly stretching out on the sofa*)
All right, that's what I do not require. I feel fine, splendid, top of the morning.

BOB
(*Cleaning desk ash tray*)
I don't get it. I thought you were the conservative, slow-to-warm-up type. Miss Birds Eye Frozen.

MARY
There *was* a rumor like that going round. Isn't it nice to know there's nothing in it.
> (BOB *empties the contents of the bookcase and desk ash trays into a wastebasket*)

94

BOB

Mary, look. What you do is none of my business. I know that.

MARY

I'm glad you know that.

BOB

(*Edging toward her, worried*)

I never wanted to see you retire to a convent. You *ought* to go out with men. You should get married again. To some man who's in love with you.

MARY

(*Listening*)

What other kind of man would marry me?

BOB

There are men and men. And—well, you don't know what you're getting into here. The idea of you sitting around necking with that bum! What the hell do you know about him?

MARY

Well, let's see. He had a very bad case of acne when he was fourteen years old.

BOB

That clarifies everything. I'm telling you this league is too fast for you, dearie. These glamour boys collect women like stamps—if you want to be added to the collection.

MARY

(*Sits up on sofa, finally speaking up for herself*)

All right. I'll tell you something. He thinks he's falling in love with me.

BOB
(*Alarmed; feeling responsible*)
He said that? Oh, that bastard! But you *couldn't* have believed him?

MARY
Why not?

BOB
Now, honestly. Does it seem very likely that that big, caramel-covered movie idol would come along and just one, two, three, bang, fall in love with a girl like you?

MARY
(*Sharply hurt, and now fighting tears*)
I guess I thought it was possible—even with a girl like me. Isn't that the height of something or other?

BOB
(*Distressed at what he has said*)
Wait, I didn't mean a girl like *you*—I meant any ordinary—

MARY
I *know* what you meant. How could you be clearer? I'm the drab, colorless type and I should know better than to believe it when somebody tells me I'm—pretty. . . .
(*She can't help the catch in her voice, try as she may*)

BOB
(*Completely unsettled*)
Are you going to cry about it?

Act Two

MARY

Maybe. Maybe. Why not?

BOB

Because you never cry.

MARY

How do you know I never? How do you know? I'll cry if I please! And I please!
(*And she lets herself go, having a real, satisfactory cry*)

BOB

Mary—

MARY

(*Flinging herself face down on sofa*)
Don't you Mary me!

BOB

(*Out   his depth and railing against it*)
It must have something to do with the position of the moon —I don't get it. Some joker tells you you're beautiful and you go all to pieces. I used to tell you you were beautiful and your detachment was marvelous to behold!
(*Leans over her*)

MARY

(*Sits up—flaring*)
You never, never, never told me I was beautiful!

BOB

Of course I did!

MARY

No, you didn't. You said you liked the way I looked.

BOB

That's the same thing.

MARY

It most certainly is not the same thing! The world is full of people that you like the way they look, but you wouldn't say they were beautiful!

BOB

Like who, for instance?

MARY

Like Mrs. Roosevelt!

BOB

(*Incredulous, entirely serio**🖤** and wonderfully maddening*)

You didn't think Mrs. Roosevelt was beautiful? My God—the character in that face . . . !

MARY

See? Now I'm a Communist. I'm picking on Mrs. Roosevelt! I *loved* Mrs. Roosevelt. And I'm not talking about character. If there is one thing I'm not interested in having any more of —if there's one thing I'm lousy with—it's character! Oh, why did you come back here tonight? I felt so good. Now I'm cold sober and everything is spoiled!

98

BOB

(*Backtracking*)
I see that you're upset. I'm sorry if I—

MARY

You're not sorry. You're merely embarrassed.

BOB

What I *am* is surprised. I never thought I'd find you sobbing on the sofa. For all the world like any other woman. Actually, it's quite becoming.
(*Sits near* MARY *and offers his handkerchief*)

MARY

(*Taking it and wiping her eyes*)
Thank you. I'm so relieved to know that.

BOB

Funny you never cried in the whole five years we were married.

MARY

I figured you were sensitive enough for both of us. You decided right at the beginning that I was the airy type—impervious to wind and weather and small disappointments.

BOB

You make it sound as though I invented your character. For that matter, what's wrong with being the airy type?

MARY

(*Getting up*)

It got to be a bit of a strain. I felt like I was on some damn panel show, twenty-four hours a day. Smiling, affable, humming little snatches of song. Laughing when I didn't know the answers. But affable, affable, affable! You don't know how I longed to get up some morning and feel free for once to be depressed, to be constipated, to be boring.

(*Pause*)

All right. I was boring.

BOB

No, you were not boring. It's strange we talked so much without communicating.

(*The fact has hit him, and he's considering it*)

MARY

It was hard to communicate with you. You were always communicating with yourself. The line was busy.

BOB

(*Surprised*)

Is that the way it seemed to you?

MARY

It seemed to me that you were taking your emotional temperature six times a day. I could almost hear you asking yourself: "Am I nervous? Am I tense? Did that upset me?" How are you feeling right now?

(BOB *almost doesn't hear this last thrust. He is seriously and soberly thinking back.* MARY *picks up the sheet and blanket*)

100

BOB

You're right, of course. I do have a bad habit of asking myself questions—silly questions. But—am I nervous, am I tense? That's more or less reasonable.

(*Looking at her*)

It was really more foolish than that. I used to ask myself—why doesn't she love me?

MARY

(*Shocked, unbelieving*)

You asked yourself—that?

BOB

All the time.

MARY

(*Throws bedclothes on sofa, exploding*)

That's why I hate intellectuals! They're all so dumb!

BOB

What kind of a statement is that?

MARY

An idiotic statement. I should save my breath and remember that I'm talking to the most sensible man in the western hemisphere.

BOB

Why do you harp on that? I'm not all that sensible.

MARY

But you are! You lead a sensible life. You eat a sensible breakfast. You limit yourself to one pack of cigarettes a day—no more than two cocktails before dinner. You're even sensible about sex.

BOB

Would you like to explain that crack?

MARY

Any man that would tap his wife on the shoulder at eleven o'clock and say "Are you in the mood tonight—because if you're not, I'm going to take a sleeping pill" is just about as sensible as you can get!

BOB
(*Blanching*)
Of course, I don't have Mr. Dirk Winston's technique in these matters.

MARY

No, you don't, more's the pity.

BOB

Look, I didn't mean to bring out your heavy artillery. I merely wanted to save you—

MARY

From what? From Dirk? But I don't want to be saved.

BOB

Just a minute. Surely you—

MARY

If he's just toying with my affections, okay. Maybe I'm in the mood to have my affections toyed with.

Act Two

BOB

Mary, I promise you—you don't have the whole picture—

MARY

But I've seen the previews. And there's not one thing in this whole world you can do about it.
(*Going toward the bedroom*)

BOB

(*Starts to follow her, but stops to steel himself*)
Mary, I'm ashamed to tell you this, but I think I just *have* to—

MARY

(*Fiercely*)
No, you don't have to, and you're not going to! I won't listen. I had a lovely time—a lovely time, do you hear? And you're not going to spoil it for me! Good night!
(*She stomps off into the bedroom, letting the door bang behind her firmly*)

(BOB *sees* DIRK's *manuscript on sofa table, seizes it, and starts to throw it into the fireplace, then thinks better of it. He goes to his desk and picks up the telephone*)

BOB

Mr. Winston's apartment, please.
(*He fidgets, but the wait is not long*)

(*Into phone*)
Dirk? You asleep? No, I didn't call to ask if you were asleep. I'm coming down there. I've got to talk to you.
(*Pause to listen*)

Who's there with you—your agent? Is she pretty? Oh, all right, all right. I believe you. Then you've got to come up here. . . . You make it sound like I was asking you to drive to New Rochelle. It's only one flight up. No, it won't keep until Monday. Listen, it'll only take five minutes—okay, okay.
(*Hangs up*)

(MARY *appears from the bedroom with an alarm clock.* BOB *crosses quickly away from the phone*)

MARY
(*Coolly*)
Do you want the alarm or shall I keep it?

BOB
You can keep it. I'm hardly likely to oversleep on that damn sofa. I'm lucky if I get to sleep.
(*Turning off one of the lights*)

MARY
All right. I'll take the sofa. It doesn't bother me.

BOB
(*Quickly, alarmed that she'll still be on hand when* DIRK *arrives*)
No, no, absolutely not. That's out of the question. Now if you're going to bed, would you go to bed?
(*He starts pacing to the window and back to the bar table*)

MARY
(*Crossing casually to the alcove bookcase*)
What's the matter with you? What are you pacing up and down like that for?

104

> BOB

(*Stops pacing*)
I'm waiting for you to go, instead of which—what are you doing?

> MARY

Looking for something to read.

> BOB

The place is full of books. What do you want?

> MARY

I want something guaranteed not to improve my mind.
> (*Glancing at books*)
The Gathering Storm . . . The Riddle of Rilke . . .
> (*Spies* DIRK's *manuscript on the desk*)
Oh. Dirk's book. The very thing.
> (*She starts for the bedroom, slowing down as
> her interest is caught by something in the manu-
> script*)

> BOB

Okay, now. Will you go to bed?

> MARY

> (*Slightly puzzled by his urgency*)
I'm going. I'm going.
> (*Taking her suitcase with her, she goes into the
> bedroom and closes the door*)

> (BOB *breathes a sigh of relief, goes to the main
> door, opens it slightly so that* DIRK *will not have
> to ring, then returns to finish making himself a*

drink. At just this moment Dirk *can be seen
arriving in the corridor. As he is about to put his
finger to the bell,* Bob *notices and dives for the
door*)

BOB

Don't push that damn buzzer!

DIRK

What's the problem?

BOB

I simply don't want Mary to hear that bell.

DIRK

Shall I come in?

BOB

Yes, of course.
> (*Drawing him into the room, slightly away from
> bedroom door. Suddenly he is awkward and nerv-
> ous in this new situation*)

Listen, can I make you a drink?

DIRK

No, I don't want a drink. I merely want to know why you
hauled me up here in the middle of the night.

BOB

Actually, it's only two o'clock. The thing is, I thought that
we should—really, what I mean is that I should—
> (*Doesn't know how to begin*)

You're sure you don't want a drink?

Act Two

DIRK

Positive.

BOB

(*After staring at him helplessly for a second*)
Well, I want a drink.
(*Goes and gets the one he was making*)

DIRK

All right. Let's have it.

BOB

(*Gulping a shot, and taking the plunge*)
Look here, Winston . . . you know damn well that all this talk about you and Mary—and my publishing your book—was supposed to be a joke.

DIRK

I thought it was funny.

BOB

Okay, you knew I wasn't serious. Then why—why—?

DIRK

Ah, but you *were* serious! You had the wild-eyed look of a man who knows he has just spoken a true word in jest.

BOB

Look, I shot off my face. A bad habit I must nip in the full bloom. However, I wish to make it absolutely clear that I never intended at any time to make a deal with you involving Mary.

107

DIRK

And I thought it was an admirable plan! You wouldn't have been losing a wife, you'd have been gaining an author.

BOB

But you've got the whole thing straight now?

DIRK

Certainly.

BOB

(*Relieved*)

I never dreamt that you were *this* anxious to get into print. And I certainly never thought that Mary—of all people—would sink into girlish incoherence at her first exposure to an actor.

DIRK

Why do you say "of all people—Mary"?

BOB

Because she's got some sense. That she could swallow that corny line!

DIRK

Do you describe everything you don't understand as corny?

BOB

What do you mean?

DIRK

Nothing. I suppose it's all right for me to go now—or did you have some other little confidence to tell me?

BOB

No, that's all. And thank you for coming. You can see I had to clear this up. I'll make your excuses to Mary in the morning.

DIRK

You will what?

BOB

I'll tell her you had to go back to Hollywood—for retakes, or whatever people go back to Hollywood for.

DIRK

And why will you tell her that?

BOB

Well, you don't think you'd be doing her a kindness to continue this little farce?

DIRK

I'm not interested in doing her a kindness. And I *am* going to see her.

BOB
(*Not understanding at all*)
But why? I thought we understood each other. I thought we talked things out!

DIRK

Yes, and you listened very carefully to every word you had to say.

BOB

What do you mean by that?

DIRK

I mean you should take that paper bag off your head. You notice everything but the obvious. What kind of a jerk are you? How dare you suppose that Mary is some kind of a charity case? Where do you get off to suggest that any man who's interested in her has to have three ulterior motives?

BOB

(At *a real loss now*)
I don't think *that*. I never thought—

DIRK

Well, you gave a very good imitation of somebody who thought that. What I told Mary may well have sounded corny. It seems that I lack literary qualities everywhere.
(*Levelly*)
But it wasn't a line.
(BOB *sinks into the chair at his desk, confused*)
You know, talking to you, I begin to see why Mary is so shy.

BOB

(*Aghast*)
Mary? *Shy?*

DIRK

That's right. Shy *and* insecure. You probably don't believe that, either, even though you're at least two-thirds responsible.

110

Act Two

BOB

(*He can't be hearing anything right*)
How could I be responsible?

DIRK

I don't know. My guess is that you treated her as though she
were intelligent.

BOB

She *is* intelligent.

DIRK

(*Waving it aside*)
Shhh! She'll hear you!
(*Going toward door, pausing to size him up*)
Where did you get the habit of making assumptions based
only on assumptions? Was your father a lawyer?

BOB

(*Staring at him*)
I'll put it all in a letter.

DIRK

All right. Before I go, I want to say only one thing. Leave her
alone. Just leave her alone. Okay?
(BOB *isn't grasping*)
I mean—*tonight*.
(*With a gesture to the sofa*)

BOB

(*Rising as this penetrates, dumfounded*)
Are you nuts? I'm getting married in two weeks!

111

DIRK

Dandy. I'll send you a pair of book ends.

(*He leaves. BOB follows him to the door and angrily shoots the bolt. He turns out the hall light, takes off his jacket, picks up the sheet, then throws it down and starts for the bedroom door. He starts to knock on it, but doesn't. Biting his lip, he looks around the room, sees the telephone. With an inspiration, he hurries to it*)

BOB

Operator? Would you ring this number for me? My number. Thank you.

(*He hangs up until the phone rings. Then he waits until it stops ringing after three rings. Picks it up*)

Mary? This is Bob. I'm in the living room.

(*Pause, while he listens for her to speak. Then the bedroom door whips open and MARY appears in the doorway, in pajamas, with the bedroom receiver in her hand*)

MARY

My God, you *are* in the living room!

(*Stares at receiver in her hand, then at him*)

What do you want?

(*Holds up one finger, getting into the spirit of the thing, and is repeating her question into receiver as she returns to the bedroom*)

What do you want?

BOB

(*Exasperated now, into phone*)

Oh, stop it! Hang up! You're just trying to make me feel foolish!

MARY

(*Appearing in bedroom doorway again, with receiver*)

I'm trying to make *you* look foolish! Who called who from the living room?

BOB

Well, I wasn't going to go barging into your bedroom!

(*He hangs up his phone*)

I had something to say to you and there seemed to be no reason why I couldn't say it on the telephone.

MARY

(*Turning to go*)

I'll go back in. You call me again.

BOB

Stay right there!

(MARY *merely reaches into the bedroom to hang up her receiver*)

This won't take one minute. I just feel—in all fairness—that I have an obligation to tell you—

(*It's a struggle for him, but he's game*)

—that I was wrong, apparently, about Mr. Winston.

MARY

And by what curious process did you arrive at this conclusion?

BOB

I talked to him. He was just up here.

MARY
(*Her eyes popping*)
He *wasn't*—you *didn't*—!

BOB

It was all right. Don't worry.
(*Facing her*)
He merely told me that I was an insensitive clunk who never appreciated you.

MARY

And what did you say?

BOB

Oh, a number of stupid things. It was not my finest hour. Of course, when he says I didn't appreciate you, that's hogwash. I appreciated you, all right.
(*Sits on the sofa*)
I just wasn't able to handle you.

MARY
(*Softened by* BOB's *direct attitude and drifting into the room*)
Don't reproach yourself. I didn't win any prizes for the way I handled you. It takes at least one to make a marriage.

BOB

Do you know how helpless you feel if you have a full cup of coffee in your hand and you start to sneeze? There's nothing to do but just let it splash. That's how I feel in all my relationships any more. Helpless—unable to co-ordinate—splashing everybody.

MARY

You're just tired.
>   (*Without thinking about it, they seem to have
>   drifted into a perfectly familiar domestic situation*)

BOB

Listen, you should have heard my various exchanges with Winston today! And thank God you didn't! Talk about a comedy of errors! I try to grasp all sides of the picture. Nobody believes that—but I try.

MARY

Bob, honey—I mean, Bob—I believe it. I certainly believe it. I honestly think you're so busy grasping all sides of the picture that you never stand back and see it.

BOB
>   (*Willing to consider this*)
Okay. Give me an example.

MARY

All right. I've been reading Dirk's book. I haven't got very far, but I think it's good.

BOB

Come on now—

MARY

No, you're going to let me finish. It may not win a Pulitzer prize, but it's readable. It's so nice and gossipy. I think it would sell.

BOB

I never said it wouldn't sell. I said I didn't want to do it.

MARY

But why not?

BOB

Oh, we've had this out a hundred times.

MARY

Bob, you won't believe this but I'm glad you have standards. I wouldn't want you to settle for trash. But it's no crime to stay in business. You've got to keep the shop open or you won't be there when a masterpiece comes along.

(*Quickly*)

Let me get it.

(*She dodges briefly into the bedroom for the manuscript, talking as she does, while* BOB *sits and stares at her*)

I'm willing to make you a small bet that you can open it at any page at all and find something that's—nice, interesting.

(*Coming back and sitting at one end of the sofa. The atmosphere is casual and they are, for all intents and purposes, man and wife at home alone*)

Maybe it goes to pieces at the end, but I wouldn't know about that. Okay, we'll just open it anywhere.

(*Reading from manuscript*)

Act Two

". . . Starlets have a reputation for being dumb only because they have such blank expressions. And the smarter they are, the blanker they look, because they've learned that it's impossible to register any emotion without using some muscle which, in time, will produce a wrinkle. Even to look a tiny bit puzzled causes twin lines over the bridge of the nose.

> (*Glancing at* BOB *to do the expression for him; it strikes her as amusing.* BOB *is simply looking at her. She goes on*)

By the time she is thirty, a starlet has been carefully taught to smile like a dead halibut. The eyes widen, the mouth drops open, but the eye muscles are never involved."

> (*Turning to* BOB *to explain*)

They don't smile like this—

> (*She smiles as most people do*)

See? You get all these wrinkles.

> (*Touching her forehead with her fingers to show him*)

They go like this.

> (*She lets her mouth drop open in a mechanized, slack smile that doesn't involve the eyes.* BOB *is not really hearing her as he looks at her. She becomes aware he isn't responding*)

You don't think that's funny.

BOB

> (*Forced to say something, unable to identify what he's really feeling, the wrong thing pops out*)

Haven't you got a robe?

> (*He rises and crosses away*)

MARY

(*Blank*)

What do you mean, haven't I got a robe?

BOB

(*Awkward*)

Well—do *you* think it's right for you to be sitting here in your night clothes?

MARY

(*Blowing*)

My night clothes! Good Lord, you'd think it was a black lace bikini! Eight million times you've seen me in pajamas!

BOB

We were married then.

MARY

(*Staring after him*)

Well, look at it this way. The divorce won't be final for two weeks.

BOB

(*Turns on a lamp*)

That may be precisely the point.

MARY

Oh, my, we are so proper! Do you feel yourself in danger of being compromised? Don't worry so much. If I should suddenly throw myself upon you, you could always scream.

BOB

Oh, shut up.

MARY

(*Continuing blithely*)

However, as it happens, I don't have a robe but there must be something around here.

(*Sees his overcoat on the window seat*)

Yes, here we are.

(*Puts it on; it is, of course, too big for her*)

I trust this will show my good faith and restore your sense of fitness.

BOB

And how do you think you look in that?

MARY

(*Sweetly*)

I don't know. Kind of cute, maybe?

BOB

Boy! All of a sudden you're cocky as hell, aren't you?

MARY

All of a sudden? It took months. It was work, work, work every minute!

BOB

But it's been worth it. Think of having Dirk Winston making passes at you! It must be like getting the Good Housekeeping Seal of Approval.

MARY

Um—sort of.

BOB

When you kissed him, I just hope you didn't damage his porcelain crowns.

MARY

(*Giggling*)
Well, we can't worry about everything. But never mind his crowns, let's talk about his book.
> (*Reaching for the manuscript on the sofa, secretly pleased at* Bob's *attitude*)

BOB

I refuse to talk about anything with you in that damn coat. You look like Jackie Coogan in *The Kid.* Here—take it off!
> (*Reaches for the coat*)

MARY

> (*Pretending to be shocked, as though fighting for her virtue*)

Oh, no—no—please!

BOB

> (*Starting to unbutton it*)

Take it off. You only put it on to make me feel like an idiot.

MARY

> (*Struggling*)

You're going to break the buttons.

BOB

To hell with the buttons.
> (*He finally gets the coat off—and they stand facing each other in a moment of nervous in-*

Act Two

                    timacy. Instinctively, MARY *puts her hand to the
                    top of her pajamas.* BOB *backs away slightly*)
No, that's as far as I mean to go.
                    (*Angrily*)
Now would you do me a favor, please? Will you please go to
bed?

MARY
                    (*Below sofa, unsettled herself, now*)
Certainly. But what are you so intense about?

BOB
I'm the intense type. Surely you've remarked on that before.
I'm asking myself how I feel. And I feel wretched.

MARY
What's the matter?

BOB
You know damn well what's the matter! I feel all involved
again. And I won't have it! I will not have it! I was getting
over you so nicely. I was cured. My God, I feel like somebody
who was getting out of the hospital after nine long months
and fell down in the lobby and broke a leg.
                    (*Because he is furious with himself*)
And you did it deliberately!

MARY
Did it—did what?

BOB
If you want to pretend that your only purpose in the last half
hour was to change my opinion of that book—all right!

MARY
(*Turns away, more quietly*)
But I gather I'm not fooling you—great student of character that you are.

BOB
Okay, what *did* you have in mind—curling up on the sofa, cute as all get-out in your little blue pajamas? No, I'll tell you. You were conducting a little experiment.

MARY
I was?

BOB
You wanted to see—just for the record—if Old Bob wouldn't leap to the bait like our friend Mr. Winston. You just wanted to check and see if I had any little twinges left.
(*She says nothing*)
Well?

MARY
(*Very quietly*)
I'm just wondering if that could possibly be true.

BOB
There's no reason for you to be kept in suspense. Yes, if you want to know, I do still feel twinges. God help me. Every now and then a sharp one. Now what do you say?

MARY
(*Thoughtful for a split second, then, in her perplexity, reverting to type*)

Act Two

Well, I don't know—it *sounds* like a gall bladder attack.
> (BOB *stares a second, then turns on his heel and grabs his jacket*)

> (MARY *impulsively, and now all regret*)
Bob, where are you going?

BOB
> (*Putting on his jacket wildly*)
Where am I going? Out! What am I going to do? Nothing!
> (*He struggles to get quickly into his overcoat, making a mess of the procedure*)

MARY
Bob, don't be silly! It's still snowing! You'll get pneumonia.

BOB
> (*Hurls his overcoat to the floor and storms out*)
Don't you worry your little head.
> (*Leaving the door open*)

MARY
> (*Shouting after him*)
But where can you possibly go at this hour in the morning? They'll think you're crazy—!
> (MARY *stands there a moment, her back to us. Then she slowly turns and picks up* BOB's *coat. She comes down to a chair, the coat clutched in her arms. After a second or so, she begins to recite mechanically, like a child writing "lines" as a punishment*)
I must keep my big mouth shut. . . . I must keep my big mouth shut. . . . I must keep my big mouth shut. . . .
> (*As the* CURTAIN FALLS)

END OF ACT TWO

Act Three

Next morning, rather early.

AT RISE: The stage is empty but the doorbell is ringing. The sofa is made up with sheet and blanket, but these are obviously unrumpled. In a moment MARY *comes from the bedroom, still half-asleep. She is in her pajamas.*

MARY

Bob . . .
> *(Staring at the sofa)*

Oh. He didn't come back at all.
> *(She stumbles to the phone)*

Hello.
> *(Doorbell)*

Hello. For heaven's sakes, hello.
> *(Doorbell again.* MARY *now realizes it isn't the phone)*

Oh. Excuse me.
> *(Hangs up)*

I'm coming.
> *(Before she can get to the door, it opens. It is* TIFFANY*)*

Oh, hello. Good morning. Oh—you're—I mean, you must be—

TIFFANY

(*After a moment of staring at* MARY, *without showing her surprise, she closes the door and speaks cheerily*)

I'm Tiffany Richards. And you're Mary, aren't you? Well, I'm delighted to meet you. May I come in?

MARY

Certainly. By all means. I don't know *where* Bob is . . .

TIFFANY

(*Taking off her coat*)

He's probably taking a walk. Lately I've been getting him to take a walk before breakfast. It's the very best thing for a sluggish colon.

MARY

(*Vaguely, still sleepy and not knowing where to settle or what to do next*)

Yes, I can imagine it would be.

TIFFANY

(*Opening the curtains*)

I never dreamt I'd find you here. But I'm so pleased it worked out this way. I've been dying to meet you. And it's a good thing Bob isn't here.

MARY

Why?

TIFFANY

Oh, he'd be bustling me right out the front door. For some

reason, he was determined I wasn't going to meet you. You know, you're much shorter than I expected.

MARY

(*Not bitchy*)
Of course I don't have any shoes on.

TIFFANY

It's just that Bob always makes you sound so overpowering. I expected somebody with a husky voice who said "darling" a lot. Harlequin glasses, big jangling bracelets, black velvet toreador pants.

MARY

But I do have a bracelet that jangles. I just don't wear it to bed.

TIFFANY

No, I can tell what you're like just by looking at you. I think you're nice.

MARY

Oh, dear.

TIFFANY

What's the matter?

MARY

It's so early. And you want to be frank and disarming.

TIFFANY

But what's wrong with that?

MARY

(*Going toward the bedroom, quickly and apologetically*)

Oh, nothing, nothing at all. It's just my low metabolism. I don't grasp things this early in the day. I mean, I hear voices, all right, but I can't pick out the verbs.

(*Goes into the bedroom*)

TIFFANY

(*Taking a dried apricot from the bowl*)

You probably don't eat right. My grandmother is like that.

MARY

(*Returning, rummaging through her purse*)

Oh, no. It's not possible! The way I feel and I don't even have a cigarette.

TIFFANY

Look, I wouldn't bother you, but Bob will be back and then I'll *never* get a chance to ask you.

MARY

(*Looks in the cigarette box on the sofa table*)

Ask me? Ask me what?

(*From now on MARY is making an abstracted effort to listen to TIFFANY but what she is really doing is making a methodical and increasingly desperate effort to find a cigarette somewhere around the apartment*)

TIFFANY

I guess I should warn you that I'm a very practical kind of person. People tease me about it all the time. Last Christmas, when I went to Palm Beach, everybody thought I was crazy because I took along my sun lamp, except it rained every day and I was the only one who came back with a tan.

MARY

Yes, but what did you want to ask me?

TIFFANY

I'm getting to that. Daddy always said that before you move into a house, you should consult the former tenant.

MARY

Oh.
> (*Checking the bookshelves and* BOB's *desk for a cigarette*)

TIFFANY

The person who's been living there will know where the storm windows are and whether there's a leak in the basement. Why should you spend six months finding out for yourself?

MARY
> (*At the desk, too foggy to understand*)

They don't have storm windows in this building.

TIFFANY

I'm not talking about the apartment. I'm talking about Bob.

MARY

You want to know if Bob has a leak in the basement?
> (*Her last resort*)

Excuse me—you don't have a cigarette on you, do you?

TIFFANY

I'm sorry. I don't smoke. It's not that I worry about lung cancer, but it does stain your teeth.

MARY

Well, I worry terribly about lung cancer. I also worry about shortness of breath and heart disease. But what really worries me right this minute is that I'm not going to find a cigarette.
(*Begins looking through the desk drawers*)

TIFFANY

Oh, I guess you never do find out. My cousin Harriet knew this boy for seven years. I mean she *thought* she knew him. But on the day they were married they took an overnight train to Chicago. And when they shut the door of their room-ette, do you know the first thing he did?

MARY

No, and don't tell me.

TIFFANY

Well, he picked up a book of matches, opened the cover, and started picking his teeth. Like this.
(*Demonstrates "picking his teeth" with a lid of book matches*)

(*The key turns in the front door and* BOB *enters, the Sunday papers under his arm. He stops, startled and then embarrassed to find the two girls together*)

Hi.

Act Three

BOB

(*Pulling himself together with an effort*)
Well. This is cozy.
(*Then rattled again, quick to overexplain*)
Tiffany, I should have explained to you last night that you'd
find Mary here.
(*Stopping to listen to himself*)
Of course, I didn't *know* last night.
(*Now really confused, looking at* MARY)
I suppose you've introduced yourselves.

TIFFANY

(*Rising and kissing* BOB *on the cheek*)
Oh yes, of course!
(*She goes into the kitchen*)

BOB

Good morning, Mary.

MARY

Good morning, Bob. Did you have to go without your overcoat?

BOB

At the time I thought so.

MARY

I made up your bed because I expected—
(BOB *takes off his jacket*)
What did you do?

BOB

Walked, mostly.
(*Looking for a cigarette on the low bookcase*)

131

MARY

Don't tell me you're out of cigarettes, too?

BOB

(*Patting his pockets. But they're empty*)

Yes, but you'll find some in the desk drawer.

MARY

No, I looked.

BOB

Well, did you try behind the—

MARY

Yes, and I tried the liquor cabinet and the stamp drawer.
(TIFFANY *returns with wheat germ for the fish*)
And the last refuge of all—the Chinese vase—

BOB

(*Starting his own search*)

Don't tell me I'm going to have to go trudging back out in
that snow!

TIFFANY

Just for a cigarette? Would you like some breakfast? There's
some orange-flavored yogurt.

BOB

Oh, no, no. Lord, no! Tiffany, be a lamb and fold up these
sheets. There may be some under the—

MARY

See! If you hadn't dumped every single ash tray last night I
could have found some medium-sized butts.

132

Act Three

> (TIFFANY *folds up the blanket, watching* MARY *and* BOB *feverishly search every conceivable nook*)

BOB

We must remain calm. It is statistically impossible that in this whole big apartment there isn't one single—just ask yourself: Where would you go if you were a cigarette?

> (*From beneath the cushion of a chair he brings up a battered half package*)

Look! Success!

> (MARY *runs to him*)

MARY

> (*As though cooing over a new baby*)

There! Did you ever see anything so pretty in your life?

> (BOB *is digging for matches to light* MARY's *cigarette*)

TIFFANY

But they're all squashed!

> (MARY *and* BOB *simply turn to stare at* TIFFANY, *simultaneously and incredulously. Then they turn their attention to the serious business of getting the cigarettes lighted, after which they exhale. Forgetting themselves, they speak in unison*)

MARY and BOB

Mmmm—that's *real* coffee!

> (*Becoming aware of what they have just done, they are a little embarrassed and pause awkwardly*)

133

TIFFANY
(*Looking up as she puts blanket away*)
Coffee? What's that about coffee?

BOB
(*Firmer*)
Nothing. Absolutely nothing.

TIFFANY
It must be something.

BOB
(TIFFANY *is obviously waiting for an explanation.* BOB *launches into it lamely*)
We once heard this announcer on television. It was late at night and I suppose the poor joker was confused from having to talk about so many products all day. Anyway, he started to do a cigarette commercial. He sucked in and smiled and said "Mmmm—that's *real* coffee."
(TIFFANY *does not react*)
You see, it *wasn't* worth going into.
(*Determined to be brisk and cheerful*)
All of which reminds me that I haven't had any coffee. I think I'd better start some up.
(BOB *goes into the kitchen almost too quickly, closing the door. There is a slight pause as* TIFFANY *looks at* MARY)

TIFFANY
How long does it take to have little private jokes?

MARY
What?

Act Three

TIFFANY

Never mind.
> (*She begins to fold the sheet on the sofa*)

I must stop asking questions for which there are no answers.
> (*Stops folding and looks reflectively at the sheet*)

This sheet isn't even mussed.
> (*Looks at sofa*)

Nobody slept on this sofa last night.

MARY

No. Bob was going to, but—

TIFFANY

He changed his mind.

MARY

> (*Not wanting to go into what really happened*)

That couch is a little short for him. Anyway, he decided that—

TIFFANY

—he'd rather sleep with you.
> (*She finishes folding the sheet, matter-of-factly. MARY's mouth drops open, but not for long*)

MARY

You mean—for old times' sake? No, indeed. Bob went—well, as a matter of fact, I don't *know* where he went. But he certainly wasn't here. As you will discover when you ask him.

TIFFANY

I won't ask him.

MARY
(*Looking at her*)
Because you don't believe me.

TIFFANY
No, I don't.

MARY
Tiffany, when you get a little older, you'll learn not to *invent* problems. All you have to do is wait, and real ones turn up.

TIFFANY
In a way—I think I'm just as glad it happened.

MARY
You are.

TIFFANY
Bob's attitude toward you has always been a little mysterious. I'm hoping this may clear the air.

MARY
Your theory is that he's a little bit homesick and a trip back to the old place may cure him?

TIFFANY
All right, yes. That's what I think.
(BOB *returns briskly from the kitchen, carrying a tray with coffee cups and an electric coffee maker on it*)

MARY
Bob. I'm afraid our little secret is out.

136

Act Three

BOB
(*Casually, unraveling electric cord*)
What little secret?

MARY
No, Bob, please. Tiffany *knows*. And she's being very understanding.

BOB
(*Glancing at* MARY *but kneeling to put the cord into the light socket*)
Would you care to be plainer? I'm simply not up to riddles this morning.

MARY
Certainly. I'm trying to tell you that Tiffany is glad we slept together last night. She thinks it will clear the air.

BOB
(*Hearing it, and instantly up*)
What did you say? What?

MARY
(*Blithely*)
I really must get dressed.
(MARY *goes off to the bedroom, closing the door behind her*)

BOB
(*Turning to* TIFFANY)
Did I hear her correctly?

TIFFANY
(*Offering him the bowl of apricots*)
Bob, whatever you do—please don't apologize.

BOB
(*Waving the bowl away and circling her*)
You're damn right I won't apologize!

TIFFANY
All right, but are you going to snap at *me?*

BOB
Wait a minute. You accept this as a *fact*—and you're not even disturbed?

TIFFANY
Should I be?

BOB
Well, I can think of six reasons why you ought to be. And you can't even think of one?

TIFFANY
It isn't like it was somebody new. It isn't even like you planned it. You're put back into an old situation, and you fall into an old pattern.

BOB
I see.

TIFFANY
Anybody will tell you that the force of habit is stronger than —than love, even.

Act Three

BOB

And in spite of the fact that I shack up with my ex-wife, you're willing to marry me?

TIFFANY

Certainly.

BOB

My God, haven't you got any principles, any ethics?

TIFFANY
(*Aroused, finally*)
How did my principles ever get into this? What have *I* done?

BOB
(*Turning away and rubbing his forehead violently. Then he collapses into the chair behind the desk and begins rummaging through the desk drawers*)
I've got to take some aspirin. I've got to clear my head.

TIFFANY

What's the matter?

BOB

You've heard of a lost weekend. Well, this has been a found weekend and it's worse.

TIFFANY

I'll get some water.
(*She goes into the kitchen, leaving the door ajar*)

(*BOB now brings out, one by one, about a dozen bottles of pills of varying sizes, including aspirin*)

BOB

I feel in my bones that this is going to be one little peach of a day. I've got to take something to clear my head or I'm going to goof. I'm going to make some crucial mistake.

(TIFFANY *returns with a glass of water*)

And where the hell is Oscar?

TIFFANY

On Sunday, what do you want with Oscar?

BOB

(*Taking the glass and two aspirins*)

There!

TIFFANY

Also take two of those large vitamins.

(*With a glance at the bedroom door;* MARY *is on her mind*)

BOB

Why?

(*He opens a bottle and takes out three capsules*)

TIFFANY

Alcohol works directly on the blood stream.

(*He swallows one*)

If you drink too much it lowers the white count, which is one reason why—

BOB

(*With another one in his mouth*)

No, no—don't give me the details.

(*Downs a third*)

Act Three

Now I've taken three. There. I can feel my white blood count going up already.

TIFFANY

(Suddenly noticing the bottle and picking it up)

Bob. You didn't take these?

BOB

You told me to.

TIFFANY

You idiot! These aren't vitamins.

BOB

What are they?

TIFFANY

Sleeping pills.

(Bob snatches the bottle from her and looks at it)

BOB

(To heaven in despair)

Oh, great. Great!

TIFFANY

Do you feel peculiar?

BOB

Not yet.

TIFFANY

Well, you will. We'd better get something.

141

BOB

It's not going to kill me. You have to take a whole bottle—a hundred and twenty, or something.

> (*Doorbell.* TIFFANY *starts to answer it*)

That'll be Oscar.

TIFFANY

> (*On her way to door*)

Don't sit down.

> (BOB *jumps up*)

I think you're supposed to keep walking around.

BOB

You're thinking of concussion.

> (*He drops into a chair again*)

TIFFANY

> (*Opening the door.* DIRK *appears*)

Oh—come in! You're Dirk Winston, aren't you?

DIRK

Yes. And you're—?

TIFFANY

I'm Tiffany Richards.

> (*Pulling* DIRK *into the room*)

And we've got a problem. Bob has taken some sleeping pills.

DIRK

Bob has!

Act Three

BOB

Tiffany, please! Don't turn this into a melodrama.
(*To* DIRK)
I just—

TIFFANY

(*To* DIRK, *pointing to the coffee maker*)
Do you think you could get him some coffee? I'll go to the drugstore and see if I can get some benzedrine or Dexamil—

BOB

They won't give you that without a prescription.

TIFFANY

(*Slipping on her coat*)
They'll give me something, don't you worry. I'd call a doctor, but they want to ask you a lot of crazy questions, like are you depressed.
(*To* DIRK)
You'll watch out for him, won't you?

DIRK

Like a mother. Now, don't worry.
(TIFFANY *rushes out the front door.* DIRK *wanders casually down to* BOB)
Why did you do it?

BOB

Because my life has suddenly become ashes. I didn't know which way to turn.

DIRK

Come off it. How many did you take?

143

BOB

Three. Look, I got the bottles mixed up. I thought I was taking vitamins. Any more questions?

DIRK

Yeah. Where's Mary?

BOB

(*Crossly*)

Well, the last time I saw her, she was in pajamas, so I think we may safely suppose she's dressing.

DIRK

What the hell are you so irritable about?

BOB

Because I had a rotten night! I drank too much, slept too little—

DIRK

You're not fooling anybody. You're mad as a hornet because I'm here to get Mary.

BOB

Why should I be mad? I'm delighted!

DIRK

You *sound* delighted.

BOB

Never mind my inflections. I just haven't had your training.

144

DIRK

You know, there's something very mysterious about your feeling for Mary. It's like gas. You can't get it up and you can't get it down.

BOB

(*The thought registers with* BOB *but he doesn't blanch*)

There's a touch of the poet in you.

(MARY *enters from the bedroom, dressed, and looking just splendid*)

MARY

(*Very cheery, seeing* DIRK)

Good morning!

DIRK

Good morning. You just getting up?

MARY

Oh, I've been up for an hour. In fact, I've already had a heart-to-heart talk with Miss Richards.

BOB

(*Going to the bar table*)

I've got to have some coffee.

MARY

(*Sweetly*)

And would you bring me some, please? And a Danish that's—

145

BOB

(*Mechanically, swerving from the coffee maker toward the kitchen*)

—cut down the middle, and no butter. I'll get it.

(*Goes into the kitchen, closing the door*)

DIRK

I woke up this morning thinking: What nice thing just happened to me? And it was you.

MARY

You're very sweet. And not like a movie actor at all.

DIRK

(*Pouring her a cup of coffee*)

Sure I am. Movie actors are just ordinary, mixed-up people—with agents.

MARY

I should think it would be fun to be Dirk Winston.

DIRK

It is. There are all kinds of advantages. I can go into any restaurant at all and the headwaiter will automatically bring me a large pepper mill. Doctors don't get pepper mills—or lawyers. Not only that, but the headwaiter stands right there until I use it. I don't want him to feel a failure, so I grind away. With the result that I've had too much pepper on everything for twenty years. I love the way you smile.

MARY

(*Nervous, but meaning every word of it*)

Dirk, I want you to know that I will never forget last evening. You couldn't possibly know what you did for me.

146

DIRK

Yes, but what have I done for you lately?

MARY

I'm not joking. I'm terribly pleased—and gratified.

DIRK

(*Urgently*)

Gratified, hell! I don't want you to be gratified. I want you to be interested. I want you to say it would cause you a real pang if you thought you weren't going to see me again.

MARY

Oh, Dirk, it would—it does.

DIRK

I got a call from the studio at eight o'clock. They insist that I fly to New Orleans this morning for some personal appearance stuff. That picture of mine is opening there Thursday.

MARY

In New Orleans?

DIRK

(*Nodding*)

The picture is called *King of the Mardi Gras*. That's how the great minds in publicity operate—the mayor meets me at the airport and hands me a praline or some damn thing. There's nothing I can do about it. It's in my contract. Anyway, here's the point. Why don't you come along?

MARY

But Dirk! I'm a working girl.

DIRK

Surely they could carry on without you for one week. Never underestimate the power of the *Ladies' Home Journal.*

MARY

But you just don't *do* that . . . !

DIRK

Sure you do. You call up and say that you've just had a recurrence of an old football injury. We could have a lot of fun. We could get to know each other.

MARY

But Dirk, I don't go off on trips with movie stars—I read about people like that in the *Journal-American* and I'm scandalized!

DIRK

Come on. Be rash. Fly now, pay later.
     (BOB *returns with an empty paper carton*)

BOB

Dirk, we seem to be all out of everything. Could I ask you to go down to the bakery and get a half-dozen Danish? It's for Mary.

MARY

Oh, let's have toast—anything.

BOB

No, there's nothing out there. I'd go myself, but I'm feeling so groggy.

Act Three

DIRK

(Rising and looking at his watch)
I don't *have* all that time . . .
(*And looking at* MARY)

BOB

It's right in the building. Go left after you get out of the elevator.

DIRK

Well, I started life as a messenger boy.

MARY

Oh, don't bother.

DIRK

That's all right. I have to see if they've got my luggage in the lobby anyway.
(*With a curious glance at* BOB, *then at* MARY)
Mary—think about it. . . .
(*He goes*)

MARY

I don't know who ate them, but there was a whole bagful last night.

BOB

I stuffed them in the wastebasket.

MARY

You what?

149

BOB

I wanted to get him out of here so I could talk to you.

MARY
(*Starting for door as though to stop* DIRK)
If that isn't the dumbest thing! Why should he have to—?

BOB
(*Grabbing her and spinning her around*)
It won't hurt him a bit. You know—I'd like to shake you until your teeth rattled.

MARY

Oh, come on! In your whole life you never even shook a bottle of magnesia.

BOB

Why, why, *why* would you tell Tiffany that we slept together last night?

MARY
(*Honestly*)
Look, Bob, whether you believe it or not, I said nothing to give Tiffany that impression.

BOB
(*This rocks him a little*)
Then why did she—?

MARY

I don't know. Some people have such a talent for making the best of a bad situation that they go around creating bad situations so they can make the best of them.

BOB
(*Trying to think*)
She didn't seem upset at all.

MARY
Upset? I got the impression she was delighted.

BOB
I know. I don't understand it. I don't understand anything.
(*He sinks into a chair*)
Mary, I'm so miserable.

MARY
Why?

BOB
You should know why. Look. In all the months we've been separated, have you been happier?

MARY
(*Reflectively*)
No.

BOB
Have you—ever thought we might get back together again?

MARY
(*Trying to hide the emotion she feels*)
It crossed my mind.
(*She sits near him, tentatively*)

BOB
(*After a breath*)
Would you consider it?

MARY
(*Struggling to control the relief and joy that want to come into her voice*)
Bob, do you know what you're saying? Do you *mean* it?

BOB
(*Surprisingly making no move toward her*)
I do mean it.
(*Thinking, and even turning away*)
I've been behaving like a damn adolescent—refusing to face the simple facts.

MARY
(*A little taken aback*)
What simple facts?

BOB
Look at the whole thing in sequence.
(*Counting the items on his fingers, logically*)
A—I wanted a divorce from you because—well, it boils down to something as simple as I didn't think you understood me. Okay.
(*Next finger*)
B—the minute we got divorced, I discovered what I should have known in the first place—that I'm the kind of man who has to be married.

MARY
(*Hurt now, but keeping a level tone*)
Is that what you discovered?

152

BOB

(*Going on with his explanation as though he were addressing a committee, completely unaware of the effect on* MARY)

Absolutely. This business of going from flower to flower never did appeal to me. I hate to live alone. I hate to sleep alone. I keep finding myself, at four o'clock in the morning, sitting in the bathroom reading old magazines. So—I decided to get married again. That's C. In the circumstances, it seemed the logical thing to do.

MARY

(*Taking his tone*)

I'd say so—yes.

BOB

But wait a minute. Now I discover that Tiffany really believes that I would actually sleep with one woman on the very eve of marrying another. By this time she should know me better than that. It isn't in my character. I'm really too square. But the point remains. *She* doesn't understand me, either.

MARY

(BOB *doesn't notice the acid that begins to creep into her voice*)

Okay, we've had A, B, and C. What about D?

BOB

(*Innocent, and eager to go on explaining*)

Well, I ask myself—am I walking with my eyes wide open into

153

another case of incompatibility? In five years will there be another divorce? I don't think I could face it.

(*He sinks onto the sofa, yawning*)

MARY

(*Casually, still playing along, though we can hear what's going on inside her*)

No, and there would be more alimony, too.

BOB

Oh! More alimony, more scenes, more confusion! The thing is, you and I may be incompatible, but we know all about it now. I think we should get married again. It would be the sensible, reasonable thing to do. Don't you?

(*He doesn't have to wait too long for his answer.* MARY *rises*)

MARY

You clunk. You block of wood. You're dumb—you're obtuse —you're—do you know something? I was so much in love with you that when you left I thought I'd die. That's right— big, healthy, well-adjusted Mary—I thought I might just possibly die! I used to sleep with the light on because in the beginning I'd wake up in the dark and forget where I was—and I'd reach out for you. Do you know if I saw a man ahead of me in the subway who walked like you or had shoulders like you, I used to feel faint, really faint. And you have the gall to stand there and talk to me about the sensible reasons why I should come back to you. You and your damn, stinking ABC's!

(*She starts for the bedroom*)

BOB

(*With his head blown off*)
Wait a minute—just because I try to be rational doesn't mean I don't *feel* anything—

MARY

Well, we won't really know until after the autopsy. Let me give you a little piece of advice. I think you should go right ahead and marry Tiffany. It would be more than a marriage. It would be a merger. You should be as happy as two IBM machines clicking away together!

BOB

(*Trying to salvage his dignity*)
So you're not coming back.

MARY

That's right. A—I don't want to, B—I don't want to, C—I don't want to!

(*She starts into the bedroom*)

(OSCAR *has let himself in,* DIRK *having left the door part-way open*)

OSCAR

What don't you want to do?

MARY

Oh, hello, Oscar—

(*She stops in the bedroom doorway, all passion spent*)

155

OSCAR
(*Closing the door—to* BOB)
I got your message. I'm shocked to see you looking so well.

BOB
What do you mean?

OSCAR
(*Getting out of his coat*)
The answering service said it was absolutely urgent that I get over here this morning. *Urgent* was underlined three times.

BOB
Oh.
(*An embarrassed glance in* MARY's *direction*)

OSCAR
I presumed that you were at death's door—waiting for me to draw up your will.

BOB
Of course not. It was really nothing that important. Actually it was really something minor. I mean, it could have—

MARY
(*Whirling on* BOB, *exasperated*)
Oh, stop it! Why don't you tell him why you called him up this morning and asked him to come over?
(*To* OSCAR)
He thought he'd come back and find nobody here but *me*—and he'd be left alone with me. But think of it—you're too late! The damage has been done.

BOB

(*Outraged, blowing*)

That's right! Listen to *her!* She knows my mind so much better than I do.

MARY

Oscar, when you go back over his accounts, you may deduct the amount he pays me in alimony. I don't want it. I never wanted it. I'm working now, and I don't need it.

BOB

(*Angrily*)

Oh, don't be noble, there's no necessity!

MARY

Oh, but there is!

(*To* OSCAR)

Do you realize that if this poor soul had to go on paying alimony to me, he could never divorce Tiffany? Oscar, I sat at home and waited nine long months for him to call. Well, I'm not sitting home any longer.

(*Heading for the bedroom*)

Now I'm going to pack.

(MARY *goes, slamming door behind her*)

OSCAR

Congratulations. You seem to have solved everything.

BOB

Oh, Oscar, you don't know what you're talking about! Even my problems have problems!

(*Uncontrollably, he yawns right in* OSCAR's *face, then plunges on without pausing, in the same overwrought way*)

What am I going to do? I can't marry Tiffany. She pushes in the bottoms of chocolates!

OSCAR

I never thought you would marry Tiffany.

BOB

Stop sounding like an owl and tell me what to do!

OSCAR

Get Mary back.

BOB

That's the conclusion I came to. But how?

OSCAR

Ask her.

BOB

Ask her? Last night I pleaded with her. Today I tried to be reasonable!

OSCAR

(*Quietly*)
So that's what she's so mad about?

BOB

Yeah! And can you explain to me why *that* should make a woman mad?

OSCAR

Not in the time we have at our disposal. But I can tell you you'd be better off giving her one idiotic reason.

BOB

What do you mean?

OSCAR

Tell her you want her back so you can bite her shoulders.

BOB

You try and tell her something! Do you know that she's actually convinced I never noticed she was pretty? What does she think—I just arrived in from Mars?
(*Yawn*)
I've got two eyes. Hell, she always was pretty. When I first saw her with that pale hair and that pale face I thought she looked like a lovely piece of white porcelain.

OSCAR

Did you tell her?

BOB

Are you crazy? She would have said "White porcelain—you mean like the kitchen sink?"

OSCAR

Come on, now, you exaggerate.

BOB

Exaggerate? You don't know the half of it. She thinks I'm made of cast iron. She thinks I've never felt even a pang. Like I was some sort of vegetable. Do you know why I put that stinking phone in the bedroom? Because after we broke up I thought she might call me in the middle of the night some night and I wanted to be sure that I'd hear it. And before she

159

gets out of here this afternoon I'm going to tell her about that phone. She's going to hear a few plain truths. She's not going to call me a block of wood.

> (*He starts toward the bedroom*)

She's not going to—

> (*He is stopped by the return of* TIFFANY, *who hurries in by the main door with a small package*)

TIFFANY

Darling, how do you feel now? Are you all right? Hello, Mr. Nelson. I don't know what this is but he said it would help.

> (*Gives him a small box wrapped in blue paper*)

BOB

Thank you, darling. It was sweet of you to dash out and get things.

> (*But he is plainly befuddled by his own mixed emotions*)

TIFFANY

> (*Sensing the problem*)

Bob—you have something to tell me. You've had something to tell me ever since you came in this morning.

BOB

> (*Evasive*)

What? No, I didn't—I don't.

> (*OSCAR is trying to make himself invisible by examining the fish tank*)

TIFFANY

You think you're inscrutable. You're the most scrutable man I ever met. Now, *tell* me—sleepy or no. You know, if you repress things, eventually you become devious—tell me!

BOB

Tiffany! Oscar is going to think *you've* taken an overdose of something.

TIFFANY

Don't worry about Oscar. He hasn't been surprised by anything since Truman was elected president. Tell me!

BOB

(*Trying to avoid a showdown, scarcely knowing his own mind and not up to a decision anyway*)

Tiffany—honey—please—

TIFFANY

(*Crisply*)

All right, I'll tell you. You've discovered that you're still in love with Mary.

(OSCAR *perks up an ear*)

BOB

(*Shocked*)

Did I say anything whatsoever to lead you to think that?

TIFFANY

Of course not. And you never would. You'd be much too embarrassed. You'd think it was adolescent and in rather bad taste. Instead, you were going to tell me all the reasons why it would be a mistake for me to marry you.

(BOB *is trying to shake his head "no," but she goes confidently on*)

(*To* OSCAR)

I figured it all out while I was going to the drugstore.

BOB

(*Groaning and blinking his eyes*)

No, no—not today!

OSCAR

What *are* the reasons? I'm interested even if Bob isn't.

TIFFANY

(*Systematically and incontrovertibly*)

Well, one, he's thirteen years older than I am. That may not seem important now, but in ten years the gap will seem even wider. Then, two—

(*She is just as thorough and efficient in her reasoning as* BOB *was with* MARY)

—he's a divorced man, which makes him a bad risk to start with. A girl of my age really deserves better than that. Finally, he's not a rich man, never will be a rich man, and he could never provide the Dior originals and the sable stoles that a girl of my upbringing would naturally expect.

(*She has given a good imitation of* BOB, *without sounding unlike herself*)

BOB

Nonsense! I never would have brought up that part about the money. It never occurred to me.

TIFFANY

(*Slowly, pointedly, only a shade regretfully*)

But all the rest of it—*did* occur to you?

BOB

(*Terribly embarrassed, and really fighting off sleep now*)

162

Act Three

Oh, Lord, I don't mind that I'm a bastard. What hurts is that
I seem to be such an *inept* bastard.

> (*Yawning in spite of himself*)

Tiffany, what can I say that—

> (*At this moment* DIRK *returns by the main door,
> a bag of buns in his hand*)

DIRK

I've got the buns.

OSCAR

Congratulations!

DIRK

> (*Noticing that although* BOB *is standing up, sup-
> porting himself with the back of a chair, his eyes
> are closed*)

I thought only horses could sleep standing up.

OSCAR

Bob is exceptional. We shall not see his like again.

> (MARY *enters from the bedroom with her suit-
> case and coat*)

OSCAR

> (*To* BOB)

What is the matter with you?

> (BOB *shakes his head to wake himself*)

BOB

I should have cards printed; I took three sleeping pills by
accident.

> (*He lets himself into a chair, puts his feet on
> another, and instantly drowses off*)

TIFFANY

Freud says there are no accidents. I think he wanted to pass out.

MARY

He was anticipating the popular demand. Dirk, I'll bet if I said I was coming to New Orleans with you—you'd go right into shock.

DIRK

What do you want to bet? Mary, are you . . . coming?

MARY

(*Struggling toward a decision*)

I have half a mind to. I used to be superior to this kind of thing. But any minute now I'll be too old.

DIRK

That's right, you'll be seventy and you'll have nothing to repent.

OSCAR

May I come too? She might need a lawyer.

TIFFANY

But you wouldn't go and leave Bob like that!

MARY

We could cover him with a sheet.

(*She starts to eat a bun, reflectively*)

TIFFANY

How can you be so unfeeling?

Act Three

MARY

My dear he has you. And when he wakes up he has all those dried apricots.

TIFFANY

But he doesn't have me. Not any more. We had an intelligent talk and I'm leaving.

MARY

That's my boy.

OSCAR

I wish he could hear this. I suggest you toss a coin. The loser takes Bob.
(*He gives* BOB *an urgent, if surreptitious, poke in the ribs*)

BOB

What, what?
(*Jumping up, grabbing more coffee*)
There's something important going on. I've got to stay awake.

DIRK

(*Quickly, to* MARY)
Honey, you know this plane is being met by a gaggle of city officials. That means you have to decide right now. We have to leave in ten minutes.

MARY

Yes, I realize that . . . !

OSCAR
(*Crossing to* MARY)
You understand that once you get on that plane you can't change your mind and get off at 125th Street. Now I think we should thrash this out.

TIFFANY
(*Composing herself formally on the ottoman*)
Yes, that's what I think.

MARY
Sure, why don't we call in David Susskind and have a panel discussion.
(BOB *falls asleep again*)
Oh, Oscar, I don't mean to be short with you but if I want to go with Dirk why shouldn't I?

TIFFANY
Well, for one thing, when a conservative person like you decides to embark on an indiscretion, you should practice up on little things before you fly off with a movie actor. You don't start at the top.

OSCAR
You see what she means. There's a hierarchy of skills.

DIRK
Just a minute. What makes you all so certain that I'm just a movie star on the make and that Mary is another pickup?

TIFFANY
Well, you use a cigarette holder . . . and her very own husband wants her back.

166

Act Three

MARY

He is no longer my very own husband.

TIFFANY

But he was and . . .

OSCAR

May I take this one? Remember you and Bob chose each other. Now you'd tell me that you chose Bob in spite of his faults. I'd tell you that you chose him because of his faults. What is missing in him is probably necessary for what is missing in you. Let us not to the marriage of true impediments admit minds.

DIRK

Am I hearing right? Are you suggesting that these two people stay together for mutual therapy? I haven't heard anything so dumb since my press agent told me he was getting married because it made it easier to register at the Plaza.

TIFFANY

Under what circumstances are you in favor of marriage?

DIRK

What do you mean, in favor? Marriage isn't something that has to be supported like low-cost housing or the bill of rights. It's something that happens like a sneeze . . . like lightning. Mary, I'll ask you once more. Will you take a chance? Will you come?

OSCAR

Why should she take a chance?
    (*To* MARY, *forcibly*)
You still yearn after *Bob*. I know you do.

167

(OSCAR's *stress on the word "Bob" has pene-
trated the fog, like an alarm bell.* BOB *comes to
slightly and looks around*)

MARY

Are we going to be naïve about this? Asking me whether I
yearn after Bob is about as sensible as asking a reformed alco-
holic whether he ever thinks about bourbon! What difference
does it make? I'm on the wagon for good and sufficient reasons. And I feel a lot better. Dirk, I *am* going with you.

BOB

Where are you going?
          (*To* OSCAR)
Where is she going?

DIRK

She is going to New Orleans with me.

BOB

          (*Coming between* MARY *and* DIRK)
Nonsense. I wouldn't let her go as far as the mailbox with
you.

DIRK

Look, van Winkle, you have nothing whatever to say about it.

BOB

That's what you think.
          (*Fighting hard for consciousness*)
I have something very important to say—and—I've been trying
to say it since six o'clock this morning.
          (*He teeters a bit, tries to get a grip on himself*)
Now *everybody* listen—

Act Three

> (*With them all attentive, his mind starts to go blank again. He leans against the frame of the closet door and slowly slides to the floor. He is asleep again*)

MARY

(*Worried now*)
Maybe we should call a doctor. I don't like his color.

DIRK

I don't like his color. I didn't like it yesterday. Come on Mary, let's leave Wynken, Blynken and Nod.
> (*He picks up* MARY's *suitcase and his coat*)

MARY

But what if he's really—?

BOB

(*With a supreme effort he rises*)
Wait a minute, now. It's coming to me.
> (*Crossing blindly to* TIFFANY)

Mary . . .
> (*Sees his mistake and turns blinking to find* MARY)

MARY

(*Going to* BOB *and extending her hand*)
I don't know whether you can hear me, but—good-by, Bob.

BOB

(*Focusing on* DIRK)
You are one of the chief causes of why I am so confused.
> (*Puts his arm around* MARY)

Don't you ever kiss my wife again.

MARY

Bob—you're making a fool of yourself—

BOB

(*Turning on* MARY *and pushing her toward the window seat*)

You shut up.

(*Back to* DIRK)

You leave her alone. She can't cope with a lounge lizard like you. She's got more goodness in her whole body than you've got in your little finger!

(*He looks dazedly at* OSCAR)

(OSCAR *shakes his head as if to say "No, you didn't get that right."*)

MARY

(*Moving toward the door*)

All right, Dirk—the poor soul doesn't know what he's talking about—

(DIRK *exits with her suitcase and* MARY *is following him when* BOB *summons a last burst of energy and lunges after her*)

BOB

Oh, don't I? I'm talking about you—you dumb little idiot—and you're not going anywhere with anybody!

(*He grabs* MARY *around the waist and propels her into the storage closet. The others exclaim almost simultaneously*)

MARY

Bob!

DIRK

(Re-entering. He has dropped the suitcase in the
hall)

Are you out of your . . . ?

(But BOB has quickly shut the door, and locked
it with a key. He turns to the others fiercely)

BOB

I haven't slept in nine months and I'm sick of it!

DIRK

Hand me that key. If you were in good condition, I could take
it from you.

BOB

That is an absolutely true statement.

(He walks to the window and calmly tosses the
key through it)

DIRK

What did you do that for?

BOB

I was going to swallow it, but it was too big.

(He collapses on the window seat, leans out for
some air, and almost overbalances. OSCAR grabs
his feet to keep BOB from falling out. TIFFANY
screams)

MARY

(Off)

Let me out of here this minute!

DIRK

(*Going to the closet door, calling through*)
Mary, can you hear? That lunatic has thrown the key out into the snow!
(*A big groan from* MARY, *off*)
What are we going to do?

OSCAR

Oh, the snow will melt in a day or two.

TIFFANY

In the movies, they just break the door down.

DIRK

In the movies the door is pieced together by the prop men so all you have to do is blow on it!

MARY

(*Off*)
Dirk! Dirk! Are you still there?

DIRK

(*Exasperated*)
Sure, I'm still here!

MARY

(*Off*)
Well, you shouldn't be! Go this minute!

DIRK

No!

172

Act Three

MARY

(*Off*)

Please, Dirk! Those people will be waiting. The studio will be furious!

DIRK

Let them be furious!

(*Starting for the desk*)

I'll call them up.

(*Remembers*)

Oh, Lord, I can't even *get* them now! And if I don't show up all the columns will say I was drunk or being held somewhere on a morals charge.

(*Turning on* BOB *as if he'd like to wring his neck*)

MARY

(*Off, urgently*)

Dirk!

DIRK

(*Going to the closet door*)

I *am* going, honey. I don't see what else to do. I'll call you tonight and we'll set up something.

(*To* OSCAR)

I depend on you as the only sane member of the group to get her out of there.

BOB

Well, it's been grand seeing you. Do come again.

173

DIRK

(*To* TIFFANY *and* OSCAR, *ignoring* BOB)
Good-by. Where's my damn book?
(*He sees it and starts for it*)

BOB

(*Snatching up the manuscript*)
What are you talking about? You offered this book to me.
You can't take it back.

DIRK

You said it stank.

BOB

I did not. I said it wasn't punctuated. I'll punctuate it.
(*Weaving toward the window seat*)

OSCAR

(*To* DIRK)
You'd better let him keep it or he'll throw it out in the snow.

DIRK

And I left Hollywood and came to New York because I
wanted to be among intelligent people!
(*Getting into his coat with a sigh*)
You know I made three pictures for Cecil B. De Mille and he
once said to me: "If you want to get hold of a woman, don't
talk to her—get hold of her—pick her up and carry her away."
I thought to myself: "This man is a jerk."
(*With a glance toward heaven*)
Cecil, forgive me.
(DIRK *exits.* OSCAR *picks up a telephone book*)

174

Act Three

> **BOB**
>> (*Forcing himself to snap to, and going to the closet door*)

Mary! Mary!
>> (*Knocks*)

> **TIFFANY**

You don't suppose *she's* fallen asleep?

> **BOB**

No, I suppose she's too mad to talk.

> **OSCAR**
>> (*At the desk, opening the classified section of the phone book*)

Why don't you try calling a locksmith? Just start with the A's. . . .
>> (*TIFFANY is picking up her coat*)

> **TIFFANY**

I'd stay if there was anything I could do.

> **BOB**
>> (*Blinking*)

Oh—Tiffany.

> **TIFFANY**
>> (*Holds out her hand*)

Good-by.

BOB

Good-by.
> (*They shake hands. He helps her on with her coat*)

Tiffany, you really are a very sweet girl.

TIFFANY

Yes, I am.
> (*Turning to* OSCAR)

Good-by, Mr. Nelson.

OSCAR

Good-by, my dear. If you're ever looking for a job, I have a large law office and could always use a girl like you.

TIFFANY

Thank you.
> (BOB *is now dialing a number from the phone book*)

OSCAR

> (*Following* TIFFANY *toward the door*)

You're not too upset, are you?

TIFFANY

Oh, I'll be upset tomorrow, when the novocain wears off. But even tomorrow I think I'm going to feel it's just as well.

OSCAR

Why?

TIFFANY

I was attracted to Bob in the first place because he wasn't attracted to me. That intrigued me. I don't want to sound

176

conceited but when you're twenty-one and you're sort of pretty and very rich, you get used to men falling in love with you. But now I ask myself—is it enough that a man is *not* attracted to you? Good-by.

> (*She goes*)

BOB

> (*On the telephone*)

Is this the locksmith? I've got a woman locked in here. Certainly I know the woman. Could you come right over? I know it's Sunday. Okay, so it's extra. Ninety-one East Seventy-first Street.

> (*To* OSCAR, *who is getting into his coat*)

He'll be right over.

OSCAR

Good. Then I may safely take my departure.

BOB

> (*Rising, in terror*)

Oscar—you wouldn't leave me alone with her?

OSCAR

You'll have the locksmith.

BOB

What will I say?

OSCAR

As little as possible.

> (*He starts out*)

BOB

> (*Clutching* OSCAR *by the arms*)

Please stay.

177

OSCAR

No, my dear boy. This dismal scene you needs must act alone.

BOB

Do you think she'll take the next plane after him?

OSCAR

Well, there are other rooms, other keys.

BOB

(*Reeling a little, but steadying himself*)
You're a big help.

OSCAR

All my clients tell me that. I'll call you tomorrow.
(OSCAR *goes*)

(BOB, *left alone, goes nervously to the closet
door*)

BOB

Mary? Mary, please answer me.
(*He kneels down and calls through the keyhole*)
The locksmith is coming—
(*The closet door opens unexpectedly and* MARY
*appears. She walks past him into the room. He
blinks*)
How did you get the door open?

MARY

My keys.
(*Shows them*)

178

Act Three

BOB
(*Rising*)
You mean you could have . . . ?

MARY
Yes. I could have.

BOB
(*Shaking himself, then nodding vaguely*)
I know I behaved like a slob . . . doing this.

MARY
Like a slob.

BOB
I made a spectacle of myself.

MARY
You certainly did. It was the silliest thing I ever saw. And do you know what? I was so proud.

BOB
(*It's all getting through to him*)
Mary! My sweet, beautiful darling. I always thought you were beautiful. I thought you were as beautiful as—a piece of white porcelain.

MARY
White porcelain? You mean like—
(*She catches herself*)
Oh, that's very sweet.

179

>   (*He goes to her and takes her in his arms, her
>   head on his shoulder*)

I missed your shoulder more than anything.

BOB

A hundred times I would have crawled on my hands and knees
to Philadelphia, but I was afraid—Mary, come home.

MARY

I'm home.

>   (*They kiss. As they do,* BOB *begins to go slack
>   again, sinking slowly onto the sofa*)

BOB

Oh, Mary, what am I going to do?

MARY

>   (*Sitting next to him as he stretches out help-
>   lessly*)

Why, what's the matter, darling?

BOB

I'm falling asleep again.

MARY

>   (*She lifts his legs onto her lap*)

That's all right.

BOB

Yeah. But how will we get those colored lights going?

Act Three

MARY

We'll manage.
> (*She starts to take off his shoes and, smiling,* BOB *falls asleep as the* CURTAIN FALLS)

END OF PLAY

E10

The hilarious smash-hit play by the author of *Please Don't Eat the Daisies* is now in print. All of Mrs. Kerr's rapid-fire wit, some of which is obscured by laughter when the play is done on the stage, is now available to the reading public.

MARY, MARY is the funny and touching story of a divorced couple who have never fallen out of love. At curtain's rise, Bob, the ex-husband, is about to marry a young, rich, and uninhibited diet-faddist named Tiffany Richards. Complications set in almost immediately when he learns that he and his publishing house are going into the red. His friend and tax-lawyer summons Mary, the ex-wife, to help them go through cancelled checks dating back to the time of their marriage in the hope of finding some deductible expenses.

With the arrival of the irrepressible, wise-cracking Mary on the scene, tax